Contents

Introduction

Adobe Photoshop software is an image-editing program that lets you create and produce high-quality digital images. The program contains a large number of editing tools and special effects capabilities that let you manipulate scanned images, slides, and original artwork.

The ability to work with multiple layers gives you the flexibility to isolate various parts of an image for experimentation and easy editing. As a production tool, Adobe Photoshop produces high-quality color separations and halftones that you can print using numerous printing options.

Prerequisites

Before beginning to use Adobe Photoshop, you should have a working knowledge of your operating system and its conventions, including how to use a mouse and standard menus and commands, and how to open, save, and close files. For help with any of these techniques, please see your Macintosh® or Windows® documentation.

About Classroom in a Book

Adobe Photoshop Classroom in a Book is designed for users at many levels. If you're new to Adobe Photoshop, you'll learn all the important fundamental concepts and features you'll need to know to master the program. If you've been using Adobe Photo-

shop for a while, you'll find *Classroom in a Book* teaches many advanced features including tips and techniques that are included with the latest version of Adobe Photoshop.

Each lesson and project concludes with a review section summarizing what you've covered. Taking time to read over the review sections will help you retain important concepts about the lesson and about Photoshop.

System requirements

Classroom in a Book can be used on a Macintosh® or on a PC that runs Windows®. In addition to the system requirements for either system, you need the Adobe Photoshop 4.0 program and a CD-ROM drive to use the Classroom in a Book files.

Macintosh system requirements

To use Adobe Photoshop, you need the following hardware and software:

• An Apple® Macintosh computer with a 68030 processor (or later model) or a Power Macintosh

• At least 16 MB of random-access memory (RAM) available for the application

• Apple system software 7.1 or later (7.1.2 for Power Macintosh). Adobe Photoshop 4.0 won't run under System 6.

- A color monitor with an 8-bit (256-color) or better video display card

- A hard drive with at least 25 MB of free space. You'll need additional disk space if you work with very large image files.

- A CD-ROM drive

For the best performance, Adobe Systems recommends the following hardware and software:

- A Power Macintosh

- Apple system software 7.5 or later

- At least 32 MB of RAM

- A 24-bit (millions of color) video display card

- A Macintosh-compatible scanner

- A PostScript® printer

- Acceleration products bearing the **Adobe** *charged* logo

Adobe Photoshop performance improves with more RAM, faster CPUs, and faster and larger hard disk drives.

Windows system requirements

To use Adobe Photoshop, you need the following hardware and software:

- An Intel® 80486, Pentium®- or Pentium Pro -based or faster PC

- Microsoft ® Windows® 3.1 with MS-DOS® 5.0 or later, Windows 95, or Intel-based Windows NT™ version 3.5.1 or later

- At least 16 MB of random-access memory (RAM) available for the application

- A hard drive with at least 25 MB of free space. You'll need additional disk space if you work with very large image files.

- An 8-bit (256-color) display adapter card

- A mouse or other compatible pointer device

- A CD-ROM drive and a sound card (required to use the Adobe Photoshop CD-ROM Set)

For the best performance, Adobe Systems recommends the following hardware and software:

- A Pentium or Pentium Pro processor

- Windows 95 or Windows NT 3.5.1 or later

- At least 32 MB of RAM

- A 24-bit (millions of color) video display card

- A PostScript printer

- Acceleration products bearing the **Adobe** *charged* logo

Adobe Photoshop performance improves with more RAM, faster CPUs, and faster and larger hard disk drives.

Adobe Photoshop Classroom in a Book package contents

The *Adobe Photoshop Classroom in a Book* package includes the following software and documentation:

• The *Adobe Photoshop Classroom in a Book* CD-ROM consisting of the lesson and project files, the Adobe Photoshop Tutorials, the Electronic Publishing Guide, Acrobat Reader software, and handouts in PDF.

• *Adobe Photoshop Classroom in a Book*

Getting started

If you haven't already done so, install the Adobe Photoshop program. The *Getting Started* guide that comes with Adobe Photoshop 4.0 includes complete instructions for installing Adobe Photoshop.

If you've never used Photoshop before, it may be helpful to first go through the Adobe Photoshop Quick Tour on page 5 of the *Adobe Photoshop User Guide*. For an overview of what you can do with Photoshop, watch the 5-minute tour movie on the Tutorial CD.

Copy the *Classroom in A Book* files

The Classroom in a Book CD-ROM disc includes folders containing all the electronic files for the Classroom in a Book lessons. Each lesson has its own folder. You must install these folders on your hard disk to use the files for the lessons. To save room on your hard disk, you can install the folders for each lesson as you need them.

To install the *Classroom in a Book* folders for Macintosh:

1 Create a folder on your hard disk and name it Adobe Photoshop CIB.

2 Drag the Lessons folder from the CD-ROM into the Adobe Photoshop CIB folder.

To install the *Classroom in a Book* files for Windows:

1 Insert the Adobe Photoshop Classroom in a Book CD-ROM into your CD-ROM drive.

2 Create a subdirectory on your hard disk and name it PS4_CIB.

3 Copy the Lessons folder into the PS4_CIB subdirectory.

Other resources

Classroom in a Book is not meant to replace documentation that comes with Adobe Photoshop. Only the commands and options used in the lessons are explained in this book.

For comprehensive information about all of the program's features, refer to the *Adobe Photoshop User Guide* or to the Adobe Photoshop online help. You will also find the Quick Reference Card packaged with Adobe Photoshop a useful companion as you work through the lessons in this book. An online version of the Quick Reference Card is included in the online help.

Restoring default preferences

The Preferences file controls how palettes and command settings appear on your screen when you open the Adobe Photoshop program. Each time you quit Adobe Photoshop, the position of the palettes and certain command settings are recorded in the Preferences file.

To ensure that the tools and palettes function exactly as described in each lesson, delete the Preferences file before you begin each lesson.

To quickly locate and delete the Photoshop Preferences file, create an alias (Macintosh) or a shortcut (Windows) for the Preferences folder.

To delete the Photoshop preferences file on the Macintosh:

1 Locate the Adobe Photoshop 4.0 Prefs file in the Preferences folder in the System folder.

If you can't find the file, choose Find from the desktop File menu, enter **Adobe Photoshop 4.0 Prefs** in the text box, and click Find.

Note: If you still can't find the file, you probably haven't started Adobe Photoshop for the first time yet. The preferences file is created when you start the program.

2 Drag the Adobe Photoshop 4.0 Prefs file to the Trash.

3 Choose Special > Empty Trash.

To delete the Photoshop preferences file in Windows:

Delete the PHOTOS40.PSP file in your Windows directory.

Important: If you want to save the current settings, rename the Adobe Photoshop 4.0 Prefs file rather than throwing it away. When you are ready to restore the settings, change the name back to Adobe Photoshop 4.0 Prefs (Macintosh) or PHOTOS4.PSP (Windows) and make sure that the file is located in the Preferences folder (Macintosh) or the Windows directory (Windows).

About Adobe products and services

For more information about Adobe products and services, you can use forums on CompuServe® and America Online℠, the Adobe Home Page on the World Wide Web, or Adobe's own bulletin board system.

To use the Adobe bulletin board, call 206-623-6984. Forums and availability vary by country.

To open the Adobe Home Page, from the World Wide Web, use the URL http://www.adobe.com. To launch the Adobe Photoshop Home Page from within Photoshop, with links to the Adobe site, choose Adobe Photoshop Home Page from the Balloon Help menu (Macintosh) or from the Help menu (Windows).

1

Lesson 1

The Photoshop Work Area

As you work with the Adobe Photoshop program, you'll discover that there is often more than one way to accomplish the same task. To make the best use of Adobe Photoshop's extensive editing capabilities, it's important to learn to navigate the work area first. The work area consists of the image window, the toolbox, and the default set of floating palettes, which are used repeatedly during the editing process.

In this lesson, you'll learn how to do the following:

- Open an Adobe Photoshop file.
- Select tools from the toolbox.
- Use viewing options to enlarge and reduce the display of an image.
- Work with palettes.

Restoring default preferences

Before starting this lesson, delete the Adobe Photoshop Preferences file to restore the program's default palettes and command settings. For step-by-step instructions about how to delete the preferences file, see "Restoring default preferences" on page 4.

Starting the Adobe Photoshop program

When you start Adobe Photoshop, the menu bar, the toolbox, and four palette groups appear on the screen.

Double-click the Adobe Photoshop icon to start the Adobe Photoshop program.

Opening files

Adobe Photoshop works with bitmapped, digitized images (that is, continuous-tone images that have been converted into a series of dots, or picture elements, called *pixels*). You can create original artwork in Adobe Photoshop, or you can get images into the program by scanning a photograph, a slide, or a graphic; by capturing a video image; or by importing artwork created in drawing programs. You can also import previously digitized images—such as those produced by a digital camera or by the Kodak® PhotoCD™ process.

Various ways to get images into Adobe Photoshop

For more information about the kinds of files you can use with Adobe Photoshop, see Lesson 2, "Image Basics," in this book or Chapter 3, "Getting Images into Photoshop," in the *Adobe Photoshop User Guide*

1 Choose File > Open. Locate and open the Lesson01 folder, then select Start01.psd and click Open.

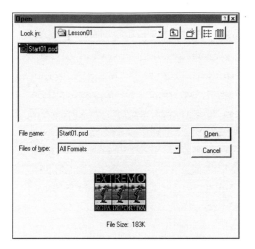

Note: The Classroom in a Book files are stored in individual lesson folders within the Photoshop CIB folder.

2 Choose File > Save As, enter the name Work01.psd; then click Save.

Using the Photoshop toolbox

The toolbox contains selection tools, painting and editing tools, foreground and background color selection boxes, and viewing tools. This section provides a brief overview of the toolbox and shows you how to select

tools. As you work through the lessons, you'll learn more about each tool's specific function.

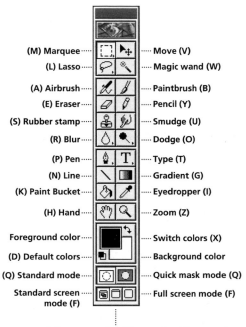

Full screen mode with menu bar (F)

Identifying tools

Because the toolbox contains many tools, it can be difficult to remember each of them when you're first getting started with the program. You can display the name of each tool and its single letter keyboard shortcut by positioning the pointer over the tool.

Try positioning the pointer over a few different tools. You don't need to click a tool to see its name; position the pointer over the tool for a few seconds and the tool name will appear.

Selecting tools

To select a tool, you can either click the tool in the toolbox or you can press the tool's keyboard shortcut. For example, you can press *m* to select the marquee tool from the keyboard. Selected tools remain active until you click a different tool.

Practice selecting tools in the toolbox using both methods.

If you don't know the keyboard shortcut for a tool, position the mouse over the tool until its name and shortcut are displayed, or refer to the illustration of the toolbox on page 11.

Some of the tools in the toolbox display a small triangle at the bottom right corner, indicating the presence of additional hidden tools.

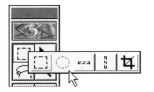

You can select hidden tools in any of the following ways:

• Click and hold down the mouse button on a tool that has additional hidden tools; then drag to the desired tool and release the mouse button.

• Hold down the Option (Macintosh) or Alt (Windows) key and click the tool in the toolbox. Each click selects the next hidden tool in the hidden tool sequence.

• Press the tool's keyboard shortcut repeatedly until the tool you want is selected.

Note: *When you click a viewing tool to change the screen display of an image, you must return to the Standard screen mode to see the default work area displayed.*

Standard screen mode

Viewing images

You can view your image at any magnification level from 0.198% to 1600%. Adobe Photoshop displays the percentage of an image's actual size in the title bar. When you use any of the viewing tools and commands, note that only the *display* of the image is affected, and not the actual size of the image.

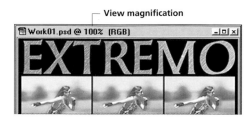

View magnification

Using the View menu

To enlarge or reduce the view of an image using the View menu, do one of the following:

• Choose View > Zoom In to enlarge the display of the Work01 image.

• Choose View > Zoom Out to reduce the view of the Work01 image.

Each time you choose a Zoom command, the view of the image and the surrounding window are resized. The percentage at which the image is viewed is displayed in the Title bar and at the bottom left corner of the Adobe Photoshop window.

View percentage

You can also use the View menu to fit an image to the screen you're working on.

1 Choose View > Fit on Screen. The size of the image and the size of your monitor determine how large the image appears on-screen.

2 Double-click the zoom tool in the toolbox to return to a 100% view.

Using the zoom tool

In addition to using the View commands, you can use the zoom tool in the toolbox to magnify and reduce the view of an image.

1 Click the zoom tool (⌕) in the toolbox to select it, and move the tool pointer onto the Work01 image. Notice that a plus sign appears at the center of the zoom tool.

2 Position the zoom tool over one of the skaters in the Work01 image and click. The image is magnified to a 200% view.

3 With the zoom tool selected and positioned in the image area, hold down Option (Macintosh) or Alt (Windows). A minus sign appears at the center of the zoom tool (⌕).

4 Click once; the view of the image is reduced to a 100% view.

You can also drag a marquee with the zoom tool to magnify a specific area of an image.

5 Drag a marquee around one of the skater's heads using the zoom tool.

Area selected *Resulting view*

The percentage at which the area is magnified is determined by the size of the marquee you draw with the zoom tool. (The smaller the marquee you draw, the larger the level of magnification.)

Note: You can draw a marquee with the zoom-in tool to enlarge the view of an image, but you cannot draw a marquee with the zoom-out tool to reduce the view of an image.

You can use the zoom tool to quickly return to a 100% view, regardless of the current magnification level.

6 Double-click the zoom tool in the toolbox to return the Work01 file to a 100% view.

Because the zoom tool is used frequently during the editing process to enlarge and reduce the view of an image, you can select it from the keyboard at any time without deselecting the active tool.

7 To select the zoom tool from the keyboard, hold down Spacebar+Command (Macintosh) or Spacebar+Ctrl (Windows). Zoom in on the desired area, and then release the keys.

8 To select the zoom-out tool from the keyboard, hold down Spacebar+Command+Option (Macintosh) or Spacebar+Ctrl+Alt (Windows). Click the desired area to reduce the view of the image, and then release the keys.

Scrolling an image

You use the hand tool to scroll through an image that does not fit in the active window. If the image fits in the active window, the hand tool has no effect when you drag it in the image window.

1 Resize the image window to make it smaller than the image.

2 Click the hand tool in the toolbox; then drag in the image window to bring another skater into view. As you drag, the image moves with the hand.

Like the zoom tool, you can select the hand tool from the keyboard without deselecting the active tool.

3 First, click any tool but the hand tool in the toolbox.

4 Hold down the Spacebar to select the hand tool from the keyboard. Drag to reposition the image; then release the Spacebar.

5 Double-click the zoom tool in the toolbox to return the Work01 image to a 100% view.

Using the Navigator palette

The Navigator palette lets you scroll an image at different magnification levels without scrolling or resizing an image in the image window.

1 Make sure that the Navigator palette is at the front of the palette group. (If necessary, click the Navigator palette tab or choose Show Navigator from the Window menu.)

2 In the Navigator palette, drag the slider to the right to about 200% to magnify the view of the skater. As you drag the slider to increase the level of magnification, the red outline in the Navigator window decreases in size.

3 In the Navigator palette, position the pointer inside the red outline; the pointer becomes a hand.

200% view of image   *View in Navigator palette*

4 Drag the hand to scroll to different parts of the image.

You can also drag a marquee in the Navigator palette to identify the area of the image you want to view.

With the pointer still positioned in the Navigator palette, hold down the Command (Macintosh) or Ctrl (Windows) key and drag a marquee over an area of the image. The smaller the marquee you draw, the greater the magnification level in the image window.

Using the Info bar

The Info bar is positioned at the lower left corner of the image window (Macintosh) or of the application window (Windows) and provides information about a file's size, resolution, view, and placement on the printed page.

1 To change the view of an image using the Info bar, drag over the number with the percentage sign at the far left corner of the Info bar.

2 Type the percentage at which you want the image displayed (you don't have to type the percent symbol); then press Return.

3 Double-click the zoom tool in the toolbox to return the file to a 100% view.

Tracking file size

By default, the Info bar displays the file size. The first number is the size of the file, and the second number (the *file size indicator*) shows the size of the file with layers.

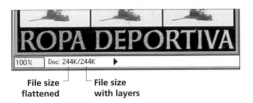

File size   File size
flattened   with layers

At this point, both numbers are the same because the Work01 file has only one layer. You'll learn more about layers and how they affect file size in Lesson 5, "Layer Basics."

Previewing before printing

You can preview the position of an image on the printed page using the Page Preview option in the Info bar.

1 Position the pointer over the file size indicator in the Info bar.

2 Click and hold down the mouse button to see the image's placement on the page.

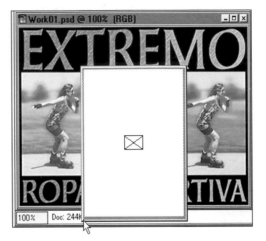

The rectangle with an X through it represents the image; the white area represents the *imageable area* (the area of the paper on which the image can be printed), and the gray border represents the *nonprintable area*. (If there is no gray border in the preview image, it's because the printer you've selected can print all the way to the edge of the paper.)

You can change the page orientation and the page size using the Page Setup dialog box.

3 Choose File > Page Setup. In the Orientation section of the dialog box, click the Horizontal option icon and then click OK.

4 In the Info bar, click and hold down the mouse button to see the change to the page orientation and to the image's placement on the page.

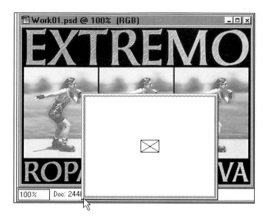

Working with palettes

By default, the Photoshop palettes are arranged in three groups, stacked along the right side of the window.

Note: Palette grouping and placement may be slightly different based on the size of your monitor.

• The *Color/Swatches/Brushes* group contains options to select, create, and edit colors and to select different brush sizes and shapes.

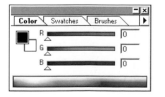

• The *Navigator/Info/Options* group contains options for viewing images and for measuring the color values in an image. In addition, the Options palette has additional controls for the currently selected tool.

• The *Layers/Channels/Paths* group contains options for adding and deleting these elements in an image.

• The *Actions* palette contains options for recording repetitive tasks, which can then be "played back" on one or more files.

Selecting palettes

Multiple tabs in a palette indicate a palette group. To use a palette, you must click its tab to bring it to the front of the group before you can select any of its options.

Click a palette tab, for example, Swatches.

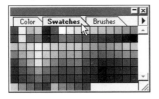

Hiding palettes

You can the hide palettes you're not using by clicking the close box in the palette. For the Macintosh, click the close box at the top left corner of the palette; for Windows, click the close box at the top right corner of the palette.

1 Click the close box (appropriate to your platform) to hide the Color/Swatches/Brushes palette.

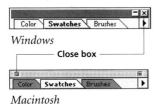

Windows

Macintosh

To display a palette after it's been hidden, you use the Window menu.

2 Choose Window > Show Color to redisplay the Color/Swatches/Brushes palette.

You can also hide all the open palettes and the toolbox with a single keystroke.

3 Press Tab to hide all the open palettes and the toolbox; then press Tab key again to redisplay the palettes and the toolbox.

Moving palettes

All the Photoshop palettes are *floating*—that is, they always appear in front of any images you have on-screen, so that you can move the palettes to see more of your image.

To move a palette anywhere on the screen, drag its title bar.

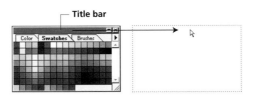

Drag a palette group by its title bar to position it under another palette. Notice that the palette group snaps to an invisible grid to align it with the other palette.

Selecting palette options

Each palette has a unique palette menu, from which you select additional options.

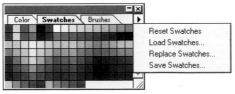

Palette menu

1 Click the Swatches palette tab.

2 Click the black triangle at the right of the Swatches palette to display the Swatches menu.

3 Release the mouse button (Macintosh) or press Esc (Windows) to close the menu without selecting a command.

Collapsing a palette

All the palettes are *collapsible.* When a palette is collapsed, only its title bar and the palette tabs are visible, thereby increasing your workspace.

Choose either of the following methods to collapse a palette:

• Click the minimize box in the right corner of the palette's title bar. (For Windows, click the box containing the horizontal line, not the box containing the *x*.) The palette group collapses. Click the box again. The palette expands to full size.

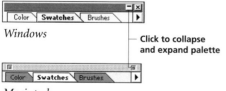

Windows

Click to collapse and expand palette

Macintosh

Note: For Windows 3.1, Windows NT 4.0, and Windows 95, make sure that you don't click the box containing the x; *clicking the* x *box closes the palette.*

• Double-click the palette tab; the palette group collapses. Double-click the palette tab again; the palette expands to full size.

(Clicking the collapse box in certain palettes produces a slightly different result than double-clicking the palette tab to collapse the palette. For example, in the Layers palette, clicking the collapse box partially collapses the palette, while double-clicking the Layers palette tab completely collapses the palette.)

Resizing a palette

Most of the palettes can be resized, with the exception of the Color, Info, and Options palettes.

1 Click the Brushes palette tab; then drag the lower right corner of the palette up about 1 inch.

2 Click the box in the upper right corner of the palette to return to its original size.

Note: If you've resized a palette, you must click the minimize box twice to collapse it. The first click returns the palette to its default size; the second click collapses it.

Customizing palettes

Palette groups can be rearranged, separated, and reorganized. If you have a small screen, you can put all the palettes you use into a single group. If you have a larger screen, you may want to separate certain palettes from their groups.

1 Drag the Channels palette tab outside its palette group.

As you drag the pointer outside the palette group, a gray outline appears.

Click the palette tab...   *and drag the palette to a new location.*

2 Release the mouse button when the gray outline appears. The Channels palette is separated from the Layers/Channels/Paths palette group.

Separated palettes

To combine palettes, drag a palette by its tab onto another group of palettes.

3 Drag the Swatches palette tab onto the Layers palette.

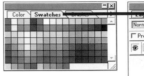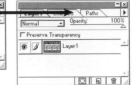

Click the palette tab...   *and drag the palette to another group.*

Merged palettes

Resetting palettes

You can return all the palettes to their default groups and on-screen positions using the Preferences dialog box.

1 Choose File > Preferences > General.

2 In the Preferences dialog box, click the Reset Palette Locations to Default option, and then click OK.

All the palettes return to their default settings and positions.

Using shortcuts

Now that you've learned the basics about how to move around the Photoshop work area, you may want to begin using some of the keyboard shortcuts that appear to the right of the commands in menus. These are especially useful for operations you perform frequently, such as displaying a specific command's dialog box.

Note: You can also define your own shortcuts using the Actions palette, which lets you assign frequently used commands to a function key or button. You'll learn about the Actions palette in Lesson 12, "Preparing Images for the Web."

You've completed this lesson. Use the Review section that follows to help you retain key concepts about the Photoshop work area.

Review

• What are two ways to select a tool from the toolbox?

• How do you select hidden tools? Identify two ways to select hidden tools.

• How many different ways can you think of to change the view (display) of an image?

• How can you preview the position of an image on the page before printing it?

• How do you select the zoom tool and the hand tool from the keyboard without deselecting the active tool? Why is it helpful to select the zoom tool and the hand tool from the keyboard without deselecting the current tool?

• How do you display a palette once it's hidden?

2

Lesson 2

Image Basics

*Whether you create artwork for display
on-screen or for print, you must understand
several basic concepts about how Adobe
Photoshop works with images before preparing your images for final output.*

In this lesson, you'll learn how to do the following:

• Recognize the difference between the two basic types of computer images—vector and raster.

• Recognize the differences between electronic images and printed images.

• Recognize three types of resolution—image, monitor, and output device resolution, and their relationship to one another.

• Work with two basic color models and learn how to measure the colors in an image.

• Recognize a variety of ways to get images into Adobe Photoshop.

• Determine the correct scan resolution for an image based on the method of final output.

• *Resample* an image, which is the process of increasing or decreasing the resolution of an image.

Restoring default preferences

Before starting this lesson, delete the Adobe Photoshop Preferences file to restore the program's default palettes and command settings. If you need step-by-step instructions about how to delete the preferences file, see "Restoring default preferences" on page 4.

Restart Adobe Photoshop.

Vector and raster images

Computers generate two basic types of images—vector and raster. As you begin working with Adobe Photoshop, knowing the difference between these image types will help you understand how Adobe Photoshop defines and interprets images.

Vector images, such as those created by Adobe Illustrator™, are composed of mathematically defined lines and curves called *vectors*. For example, a figure drawn in a vector-based program can be moved, resized, or rotated as an independent object because the program retains the definition of the figure mathematically. For this reason, vector-based programs work best for type and other shapes that require crisp, clear boundaries. To see a color sample of a vector image and a raster image, see illustration 2–1 in the color section of this book.

Raster images, such as those created by Adobe Photoshop, are composed of a grid, or *raster* of small squares, called pixels. For example, a figure drawn in a raster-based program is composed of a group of pixels in a particular location, which create the appearance of a figure. To edit a raster image, you edit a group of pixels instead of a mathematically defined object. Raster- or pixel-based images work best with photographic images or with images created in painting programs.

Digital images versus printed images

Most photographs are called continuous-tone images, because the method used to develop the photograph creates the illusion of perfect continuous tone throughout the image. Digital, or pixel-based images, like those created in Adobe Photoshop, also create the illusion of continuous tone, because each pixel can be colored independently, creating a smooth, continuous transition of color throughout the image.

Printing presses are not capable of reproducing continuous tones in an image, and so create the illusion of continuous tone using *halftone dots*. Halftone dots are rows of small, variously sized dots that create the appearance of different shades of color when printed.

To see samples of two halftone screens, one using black ink and one using the process ink colors, see illustration 2–2 in the color section of this book.

What is resolution, and how does it affect an image?

In broad terms, *resolution* refers to the unit of measurement used to determine the size of an image, the way an image is displayed on your monitor, and the device on which an image is output.

Specifically, you must consider three types of resolution when preparing images in Adobe Photoshop:

• *Image resolution* refers to the size of the file in pixels, called pixels per inch (ppi).

• *Monitor resolution* determines how your image is displayed on your monitor, called dots per inch (dpi).

• *Output device resolution* determines the quality of a final printed image, which is measured in both dots per inch (dpi) and lines per inch (lpi).

The following sections describe each type of resolution in detail, and will help you understand the relationship each of them has to the others.

1. Image resolution

Digital images are represented in pixels. *Image resolution* refers to the number of pixels in the image and is generally measured in pixels per inch, or *ppi*. The more pixels per square inch of the image, the higher its resolution, and subsequently, the larger the file. For example, a 1-inch square of an image scanned at 72 ppi contains 5,184 pixels (72 pixels wide x 72 pixels high), and has a file size of 6K, while the same 1-inch square of an image scanned at 144 ppi contains 20736 pixels (144 pixels wide x 144 pixels high), and has a file size of 21K.

To see how image resolution affects an image, you'll open two identical images scanned at different resolutions and examine the differences between them.

1 Choose File > Open, locate and select Skate72.psd in the Lesson02 folder; then click Open. An image of a skater appears at a 100% view on your desktop.

2 Choose Image > Image Size. At the top of the dialog box, the Pixel Dimensions (file size) and the width and height of the image appear.

3 Make a note of the pixel dimensions and the width and height of the image, and then click Cancel to close the dialog box.

Now you'll open an image of the skater scanned at a higher resolution and compare the differences between the files.

4 Choose File > Open, locate and select Skate144.psd in the Lesson02 folder; then click Open.

The second skater image appears larger on-screen than the first image (You'll learn why in the next section, "Monitor resolution.")

5 Choose Image > Image Size. Notice that although the print dimensions remain the same as those of the first image, the file is larger and the resolution is higher.

6 Click Cancel to close the dialog box.

7 Align the two images side-by-side on your screen, and make sure that the Skate144.psd image is the active window.

8 Choose View > Print Size. The Print Size command displays the size at which each image will be printed, which in this example is the same size.

9 Choose File > Close to close the skater files. If prompted, do not save changes.

Next, you'll discover why the second skater image, scanned at a higher resolution than the first, appeared larger on your monitor than the first image, even though the print size for each image was the same.

2. Monitor resolution

Monitors have a fixed resolution, determined by the manufacturer. Most Macintosh monitors display images at 72 dots per inch, and typically IBM-compatible monitors display images at 96 dots per inch.

The monitor's resolution determines the size of the image displayed on-screen, and should not be confused with image resolution. Because an image may have a higher resolution than the monitor on which it's displayed, an image with a higher resolution will appear larger on-screen than in print.

In this example, the first file, Skate72.psd, is displayed on the monitor in actual size—the monitor in the example displays 72 pixels per inch (ppi), and the image is scanned at 72 ppi. (For Windows, monitors usually display 96 ppi).

The second file, Skate144.psd, with a resolution of 144 ppi appears at twice its actual size on the 72 dpi monitor, because only 72 of the 144 ppi can be displayed in 1 inch on the monitor.

72-ppi image displayed on a 72-dpi monitor   *144-ppi image displayed on a 72-dpi monitor*

In addition to the resolution at which a monitor displays pixels, each pixel has a particular depth, called *bit resolution*. Bit resolution measures the amount (number of bits) of color information stored per pixel. The bit resolution of a pixel is a measurement of the amount of color information stored in a single pixel. The greater the pixel depth, the larger the range of available colors, resulting in a more accurate representation of the colors in an image. For example, a pixel with a bit depth of 1 has two possible values: on or off (black or white). A pixel with a bit depth of 8 has 2^8, or 256 possible values; a pixel with a bit depth of 24 has 2^{24}, or 16 million color values.

Illustration 2–3 in the color section of this book shows images displayed at varying bit depths.

Note: *For best results when working with Adobe Photoshop, it is recommended that you use a 24- or 32-bit monitor.*

3. Output resolution

Output device resolution refers to the number of dots per inch (dpi) that the output device produces. For example, laser writers typically have a resolution of 300 or 600 dpi, and a high-quality imagesetter can print at a range between 1200 dpi and 2400 dpi or higher.

Coupled with the dpi resolution of an output device is its *screen frequency*. Screen frequency determines the number of halftone cells printed per inch in a grayscale image or a color separation. Also known as the screen ruling or line screen, screen frequency is measured in lines per inch (lpi). The combination of resolution and screen frequency determines the detail in a printed image. For example, newspapers are usually printed with a line screen of 75 lpi to 85 lpi, while a high-quality art book might be printed at a line screen as high as 200 lpi.

For information about line screen values for various types of publications, see "Scanning for printed publication" on page 33.

Color model basics

A color model is a method for displaying and measuring color. The human eye perceives color according to the wavelength of the light it receives. Light containing the full color spectrum is perceived as white. When no light is present, the eye perceives black.

The following sections discuss two of the most common color models: red, green, and blue (RGB), the method by which monitors display color; and cyan, magenta, yellow, and black (CMYK), the method by which images are printed using the four process ink colors.

Color gamuts

The *gamut* of a color model is the range of colors that can be displayed or printed. The largest color gamut is that viewed in nature. The RGB gamut is smaller than the natural

color gamut, and the CMYK color gamut is smaller than the RGB gamut. Illustration 2–4 in the color section of this book displays a color rendering of the CMYK color gamut.

The RGB color model

A large percentage of the visible spectrum of color can be represented by mixing three basic components of colored light in various proportions. These components are known as the *primary colors*: red, green, and blue (RGB). Because various percentages of each color are added to create new colors, the RGB color model is known as *additive color*. Equal amounts of red, green, and blue produce white.

All monitors display color using a mixture of the primary additive colors of red, green, and blue. As a general rule, you should edit your color images in the RGB model for the following reasons:

• RGB files are smaller than files created in other color models.

• Monitors display RGB colors best.

• The RGB color model provides a larger color spectrum than other color models on a monitor, such as CMYK. (You'll learn about the CMYK color model in the next section on page 31.)

You'll begin by looking at an image of an RGB color model, and then you'll learn how to measure the colors in the model using the Info palette.

1 Choose File > Open, locate and select RGB.psd in the Lesson02 folder; then click Open. The RGB color model image appears See illustration 2–5 in the color section of this book for a color rendering of the RGB color model.

Now you'll use the Info palette and the eyedropper tool to measure the color information in the RGB model. When you position the eyedropper over the colors in an image, the Info palette displays the color values, depending on the color model you're working in.

2 Choose Window > Show Info to open the Info palette.

3 Select the eyedropper tool (✐) in the toolbox, and move the tool onto the image area.

4 Position the eyedropper tool over the red area of the color model image. The Info palette displays a value of 255 for red, 0 for green, and 0 for blue.

5 Position the eyedropper tool over the green area of the color model image. Now the Info palette displays a value of 0 for red, 255 for green, and 0 for blue.

6 Repeat the process for the blue portion of the color model image.

7 Position the eyedropper in the white area of the color model, where the three colors intersect. Notice that the value is 255 for each of the red, green, and blue color values, indicating that equal portions of red, green, and blue create white.

8 As a final step, position the eyedropper anywhere in the black area of the color model image. Notice the value is 0 for each of the red, green, and blue color values, indicating the absence of color.

9 Choose File > Close to close the rgb.ps file. If prompted, do not save changes.

The CMYK color model

The CMYK (cyan, magenta, yellow, and black) color model represents the four process inks used to print images on a press. To print an image on-press, each of four plates is inked with one of the colors. The plates produced for each color are called *color separations*. The combined color separations form a complete, or *composite* image. In Lesson 13, "Creating Color Separations," you'll learn much more about CMYK and about producing color separations for printing on-press. For now, you'll have a look at a file containing the CMYK color model.

The CMYK model is called *subtractive color* because combining all colors subtracts color and produces black.

1 Choose File > Open, locate and select cmyk.psd in the Lesson02 folder; then click Open. The CMYK color model image appears.

Illustration 2–6 in the color section of this book displays a color rendering of the CMYK color model.

2 Position the eyedropper tool over the cyan part of the image. In the Info palette, the cyan value is 100%, and the magenta, yellow, and black values are 0%.

3 Move the pointer over the magenta and yellow portions of the image to see the values in the Info palette.

4 Move the pointer into the black area where the three circles intersect.

You'll notice that the Info palette reflects a value of 100% for cyan, magenta, and yellow.

Theoretically, mixing 100% of cyan, magenta, and yellow produces black, but because of impurities in ink, a mixture of 100% of each of these colors produces a muddy brown. For that reason, where a rich black color is desired, you use a combination of cyan, magenta, yellow, and black ink to produce black.

5 Position the eyedropper in the black background outside the color model.

In the Info palette, you'll notice that the black value is now 100%, and the values of cyan, magenta, and yellow have decreased from 100% to lesser values.

6 Choose File > Close to close the CMYK color model file. If prompted, do not save changes.

Getting images into Photoshop

There are several ways to get images into Adobe Photoshop. You can use a scanner to scan an image, or import vector artwork from a drawing application like Adobe Illustrator. Images can also come from a digital camera or from a Photo CD. The rest of this lesson focuses on scanned images.

Scanning basics

This section provides general information about scanning techniques to help you determine the best input settings for your images.

Each scanner has its own software that controls how it works. Scanning software may be a plug-in module to Adobe Photoshop, or it may be a stand-alone application. For information specific to your scanner, consult your scanner documentation.

Before you scan

The choices you make before scanning an image affect the quality and usefulness of the resulting digital file. Before scanning an image, be sure to do the following:

• Determine the scan resolution of the image, based on the desired quality of the final output. (See "Scanning for electronic publication" on page 34.)

• On the scanner bed, define the area of the image you want to scan; then crop the area a bit larger than the actual size of the area you want. You should do final cropping in Adobe Photoshop *after* scanning.

• Determine the optimal dynamic range (if your scanner lets you set black points and white points).

• Check for *color casts* (imbalance in one or more colors) that should be eliminated during the scan.

The following sections describe how to select the correct resolution for electronic or printed images. The exercises show you two different methods for determining scan resolution.

Determining the scan resolution

The optimal resolution of an image depends on the desired output of the final image. If an image's resolution is too low, Adobe Photoshop may use the color value of a single pixel to create several halftone dots. This results in *pixelization*, or very coarse-looking output. If the resolution is too high, the file contains more information than the printer needs and becomes unnecessarily large.

Illustration 2–7 in the color section of this book shows two images, once scanned with adequate resolution, and one scanned with inadequate resolution.

Scanning for printed publication

In general, the combination of image resolution and screen frequency determines the detail in a printed image.

As you learned earlier in this lesson, screen frequency is measured in lines per inch (lpi) and determines the number of halftone cells printed per inch. (To determine the screen frequency for an image you're going to print, check with your printer.) If you plan to print your images, a good rule of thumb is to scan the image at 1.5 to 2 times the screen frequency to be used for printing.

The following table shows the typical line screen (screen frequency) and scan resolution used by various types of publications:

Publication	Line Screen	Scan Resolution
Newspaper	85–150 lpi	125–225
Magazine	135–175 lpi	200–265
Art Books	150–200 lpi	225–300

When setting a scan resolution, the goal is to balance the resolution with a manageable file size.

If you plan to print your image using a half-tone screen, the range of suitable image resolutions depends on the screen frequency of your output device. You can have Photoshop determine a recommended resolution for your image based on your device's screen frequency.

In this section, you'll look at the attributes of the Auto Resolution dialog box. You won't be entering settings for the dialog box; you'll just become familiar with how the settings work.

1 Choose File > New. Accept the default settings and click OK to open a new, blank image. (You must have a file open to use the Image Size command.)

2 Choose Image > Image Size.

3 Click Auto.

4 For Screen, enter the screen frequency for the output device. If desired, choose a new unit of measurement. Note that the screen value is used only to calculate the image resolution; it does not set the screen for printing.

Important: To specify the halftone screen frequency for printing, you must use the Halftone Screens dialog box, accessible through the Page Setup dialog box. For more information on defining halftone screens, see "Selecting halftone screen attributes" in the Adobe Photoshop User Guide.

5 For Quality, select one of the following options:

• Draft, to produce a resolution that is the same as the screen frequency (not less than 72 ppi).

• Good, to produce a resolution that is 1.5 times the screen frequency.

• Best, to produce a resolution that is 2 times the screen frequency.

6 Click Cancel to close the Auto Resolution dialog box; then click Cancel to close the Image Size dialog box.

Scanning for electronic publication

If you are preparing images for on-screen viewing, the scan resolution need not be greater than the resolution of the target monitor. However, keep in mind that on-screen images are displayed at a 1:1 ratio (1 image pixel to 1 monitor pixel), so the size of an image may vary based on the dpi of the monitor on which the image is displayed.

Scanning using the file size setting

The best way to ensure that you have all the data you need for your Adobe Photoshop image is to create a dummy file that tells you exactly how much data—that is, what file size—you need for your final output.

Using this method is helpful if you have an original image that is smaller than the final image you want to produce. For example, if you want to increase a 2-inch-by-3-inch original image to create a 4-inch-by-6-inch scanned image printed at a line screen of 150 lpi, use the file size method to determine how much data you'll need.

Now, you'll use the File > New method using the information from the previous example.

1 Choose File > New.

2 Enter the 4 inches for the width, 6 inches for the height, and 300 in the Resolution text box. (The resolution should be 1.5 times to 2 times the screen frequency you will use to print, which you've determined to be 150.)

The New dialog box displays the image size above the dimensions. The final image is 4 inches wide by 6 inches high, printed at a screen frequency of 150 lpi (hence the 300-ppi resolution, which is two times the line screen). The file size must be 6.18 megabytes.

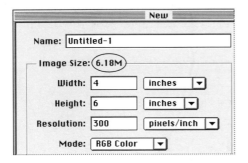

To produce the scan, enter the resulting file size in your scanner settings. (It does not matter what resolution or image dimensions appear in the scanner settings.)

Once you have scanned the image and imported it into Photoshop, use the Image Size command to enter the correct width and height for the image.

Scanning using the resolution setting

If you can't use file size as the determining factor in choosing your scanner settings, you can calculate a scan resolution using the original and final image dimensions and the screen frequency of your output device.

1 Multiply the screen frequency by 2. (two is the typical ratio of image resolution to screen frequency needed to produce a good-quality image.) For the typical screen frequency by publication type, see "Scanning for printed publication" on page 33.

2 Multiply the result in step 1 by the *size change factor* (the ratio of the final image dimensions to the original) to get the estimated scan resolution you need.

For example, suppose you are scanning an image that is 2 inches wide by 3 inches high. You want to produce a final image that is 6 inches wide by 9 inches high. You are using a screen frequency of 85 lpi.

To calculate the scan resolution, you first multiply 85 (the screen frequency) by 2 to get 170. You then multiply 170 by 3 (the ratio of the final image to the original image dimensions) to get a scan resolution of 510 ppi.

Different color separation procedures may require different ratios of image resolution to screen frequency. It's a good idea to check with your service provider or printer to finalize your requirements before you scan the image.

Resampling an image

Resampling refers to changing the pixel dimensions (and therefore the file size) of an image. In Adobe Photoshop, you can change the pixel dimensions directly, or you can change the pixel dimensions by changing either the print dimensions or the resolution while the Resample Image option is selected.

When you *sample down* (decrease the number of pixels), Photoshop deletes information from the image. When you *resample up* (or increase the number of pixels), Photoshop creates new pixel information based on the color values of the existing pixels. In both cases, Photoshop uses an interpolation method to determine how pixels are added or deleted.

Downsampling and then resampling up to the original resolution causes the quality of an image to deteriorate. This is because once an image has been downsampled, some of the original color information is lost. When Photoshop resamples the image back up, it attempts to reconstruct the image data based on the new color information. Because the added pixels are interpolated (inserted) from the new downsampled color information, the resulting image can appear blurry or out of focus. Illustration 2–8 in the color section of this book shows the effect of downsampling an image (with adequate resolution) and sampling up an image (with inadequate resolution.)

It's best to scan in or create your image using a high enough resolution so that you don't have to increase the pixel dimensions from within Adobe Photoshop. If you want to preview the effects of changing the pixel dimensions on-screen, or print proofs at different resolutions, resample a duplicate of your original file.

Sampling down the skater image

You'll start by sampling down the skater image, and then sample it back up to see how resampling affect the image.

1 Choose File > Open, select Skate144.psd from the list of files and then click Open.

2 Choose Image > Image Size. First, make sure that the Constrain Proportions and Resample Image options are turned on at the bottom of the dialog box.

Resample image
Constrain proportions

3 Type 72 in the Resolution text box. You'll notice that the pixel dimensions of the image change, but the print size remain the same.

4 Click OK. Because information was deleted from the Skate144.psd image when the image was sampled down to a lower resolution, the quality of the image remains intact.

Sampling up the skater image

Next, you'll sample up the 72-ppi image. You'll see how the image quality deteriorates when you increase the resolution after having decreased it, while maintaining the print size.

1 Make sure that the Skate144.psd window is still active; then choose Image > Image Size.

2 Enter 300 in the Resolution text box.

Notice that while the pixel dimensions increase, the print size remains the same.

3 Click OK. The image is badly out of focus, because the image was sampled back up by inserting color information from the sampled down file.

4 Choose File > Close, and do not save changes.

You have completed the Image Basics lesson. For in-depth information about all the image options, see Chapter 3, "Getting Images into Photoshop," in the *Adobe Photoshop User Guide.*

Review

• What is the difference between a raster image and a vector image?

• What are some of the ways to get images into Photoshop?

• How do you determine the resolution at which an image should be scanned?

• If you are scanning for electronic publication (versus printed publication), at what resolution should the image be scanned?

• What is screen frequency, and what effect does it have on a printed image?

• Define resampling. How does sampling up an image differ from sampling down an image?

• What is the general rule for resampling images?

3

Lesson 3

Calibrating Your Monitor

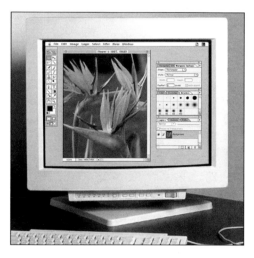

Calibration is the process of adjusting your monitor and the Adobe Photoshop color conversion settings to compensate for factors that affect both the on-screen image and its conversion to printed output. The calibration process is essential if you want to reproduce colors accurately, both on-screen and in print.

In this lesson, you'll learn how to do the following:

• Calibrate your monitor to remove any color casts and to stabilize the colors on your screen.

• Use the Monitor Setup dialog box to define settings that apply to your monitor and your work environment.

Restoring default preferences

Before starting this lesson, delete the Adobe Photoshop Preferences file to restore the program's default palettes and command settings. If you need step-by-step instructions about how to delete the preferences file, see "Restoring default preferences" on page 4.

Restart Adobe Photoshop.

About calibration

Classroom in a Book divides the calibration process into two areas—the adjustment of your monitor, called *device calibration*, and the adjustment of the printing inks and paper you use when you print an image, called *color management*. In this lesson, you'll calibrate your monitor to stabilize the colors on your screen. In Lesson 13, "Creating Color Separations," you'll complete the calibration process by specifying the properties of the inks and paper stock used to reproduce printed colors.

The monitor calibration tools included with Adobe Photoshop affect how colors appear on your monitor. Although this is true for both the Macintosh and Windows versions of Photoshop, important differences exist in the way monitor calibration affects the appearance of images on these platforms:

• The Macintosh version of Photoshop provides a Gamma control panel whose settings offer global monitor calibration. On the Macintosh, adjusting the Monitor Setup options affects how an image is displayed in CMYK mode (as it is converted to RGB color for display on the monitor) but not how the image is displayed in RGB mode.

• The Windows version of Photoshop does *not* offer global monitor calibration, but instead affects the monitor display only *within* Photoshop. The Gamma control in the Calibrate dialog box measures your monitor's behavior and then uses the result of the measurement to adjust the impact of the gamma setting in the Monitor Setup dialog box. In Windows, therefore, adjusting the Monitor Setup options affects how an image is displayed in RGB mode but not in CMYK mode.

Note: In addition to affecting how colors are converted between CMYK and RGB modes, the settings in the Monitor Setup dialog box affect the overall brightness display of all images.

Step 1: Calibrate your monitor

The Photoshop calibration tools let you calibrate the gamma, the color balance, and the white and black points of color on your monitor. These settings help you eliminate *color casts* (the imbalance of one or more colors) in your monitor display, ensure that your monitor grays are as neutral as possible, and standardize the display of images on different monitors so that images look the same with different monitor and video-card combinations.

If you are using a Macintosh computer and have a third-party monitor calibration utility installed, such as the Radius™ Calibrator or Daystar's Colorimeter 24, you should use either that utility or the Adobe Photoshop gamma tools, but not both. A third-party calibration program updates the Macintosh Photoshop color space descriptor file; therefore using both systems will miscalibrate the monitor. If you are using third-party calibration tools, see Chapter 5, "Reproducing Color," in the *Adobe Photoshop User Guide*. For Classroom in a Book, use the steps provided in this lesson.

1 Make sure that your monitor has been turned on for at least half an hour so the monitor display has stabilized.

2 Set the room lighting at a level you plan to maintain; then adjust the brightness and contrast controls on your monitor.

Because changes in these factors can dramatically affect your display, you should close off your room from external light sources and tape down the monitor and room lighting controls once you've set them.

3 Turn off any desktop patterns, and change the background color on your monitor to a light gray.

This prevents the background color from interfering with your color perception and helps you adjust the display to a neutral gray. If you need help changing the background color on your desktop, refer to the user manual for your operating system.

4 Depending on the platform you're working with, do one of the following:

• On the Macintosh, choose Control Panels from the Apple menu, then choose the Gamma control panel from the list. Use the On and Off buttons to turn the Gamma software on and off. If you turn off the Gamma software, the monitor's default values are used.

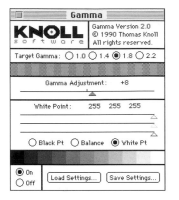

Note: *If you don't see the Gamma control panel, locate the Gamma file in the Goodies > Calibration folder inside the Adobe Photoshop folder. Drag the Gamma icon into the Controls Panels folder in the System Folder, and restart your Macintosh.*

• For Windows only: Choose File > New, accept the default settings and click OK to create a new, blank image. You'll match a piece of white paper to the white background in the blank image. Next, choose File > Color Settings > Monitor Setup.

5 Click a target gamma at the top of the control panel (Macintosh), or type a value for Gamma in the Monitor Setup dialog box (Windows). A target gamma of 1.8 is recommended for printing CMYK images, because it closely matches printer dot gain.

Note: *If you're sending your output to an RGB device (for example, a monitor, film recorder, or RGB printer), use a higher target value. Images intended for the Web or video should have a target gamma of 2.2, which is the typical gamma of most monitors and television sets. If you plan to print or display the image using another application or on another platform, use a gamma of 1.8; that value is the closest match for uncorrected gamma.*

6 For Windows only: If you changed the gamma value in step 4, click OK; then choose File > Color Settings > Monitor Setup to reopen the Monitor Setup dialog box.

7 For Windows only: Click Calibrate in the Monitor Setup dialog box. You can preview the effects of calibration on an open Photoshop image at any time by clicking Preview in the Calibrate dialog box.

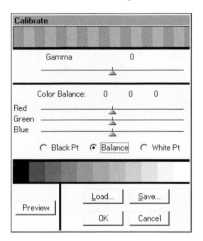

8 For Macintosh only: Once you've opened the Gamma control panel, return to Photoshop, choose File > New, accept the default settings in the New dialog box, and click OK to create a new, blank image.

You'll match a piece of white paper with the white background in the blank image to calibrate your monitor.

9 Hold up a piece of white paper next to the white background of the blank image window on your screen. (For this exercise, we suggest using a piece of plain white copy paper, simply because it's easily accessible.)

For actual work, use a piece of paper that is similar in color to the stock on which you'll print.

10 Click White Pt, and drag the three slider triangles until the monitor white matches the paper as closely as possible. This process lets you compensate for the bluish cast found on most monitor displays.

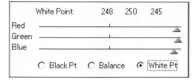

Note: For maximum accuracy, view the paper under controlled lighting, such as a light box or a combination of fluorescent and tungsten light bulbs.

11 Adjust the gamma by dragging the Gamma Adjustment slider until the solid gray areas match the patterned gray areas in the gamma strip above the slider.

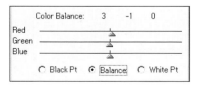

12 Adjust the color balance by clicking Balance and dragging the three slider triangles until the gray areas in the strip below the sliders become a neutral gray.

This adjustment controls the monitor's mixture of red, green, and blue; and it compensates for color casts in the monitor.

13 Adjust the black point by clicking Black Pt and dragging the three slider triangles until no color tint appears in the shadow tones in the lower strip and you can see a distinct gradation between each pair of swatches.

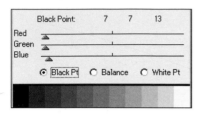

14 If necessary, readjust the color balance and then the gamma.

It's a good idea to save the gamma settings if you use different monitors or use paper stocks with different tints. To reuse the gamma settings, use the Save Settings and Load Settings buttons in the Gamma control panel (Macintosh) or in the Calibrate dialog box (Windows). You'll save the settings during this exercise so you can reload them later if necessary.

1 In the Gamma control panel (Macintosh) or the Calibrate dialog box (Windows), click the Save Settings button. The Save Settings dialog box appears.

2 Type the name Settings.psd; then save the settings file in the Lesson03 folder. Click Save to save the settings.

3 When you've finished making adjustments, close the Gamma control panel (Macintosh) or the Calibrate dialog box (Windows).

4 Choose File > Close to close the blank files you created when matching your paper stock to your monitor. Do not save changes.

Once you have calibrated your monitor, you should not have to recalibrate unless you change any of the factors affecting calibration. For example, if you change the room lighting or readjust the monitor brightness and contrast controls, you must recalibrate your system. For this reason, it's recommended that you tape down your monitor's brightness and contrast controls after calibrating the monitor, and that you maintain consistent room lighting conditions.

Step 2: Enter the Monitor Setup information

Once you have calibrated your monitor, enter your monitor specifications in the Monitor Setup dialog box. Adobe Photoshop uses the information in the Monitor Setup dialog box to account for factors affecting the monitor display: the target gamma and white point, the type of phosphors in the monitor, and the room lighting conditions.

In addition to affecting the overall monitor display, the Monitor Setup information determines how the program converts colors between modes. This means that Monitor Setup options will affect how the conversion of an RGB image to CMYK mode as well as affect the on-screen display of CMYK (or duotone) colors (Macintosh) or RGB images (Windows). If you change these settings after you have converted an image to CMYK mode, *only* the display is affected. You must revert to the original RGB mode and then reconvert the image to CMYK mode for these changes to affect the separation data. (See Lesson 13, "Creating Color Separations," for information about generating color separations.)

1 Choose File > Color Settings > Monitor Setup.

2 For Monitor, select the monitor you are adjusting. If your monitor is not listed as an option, choose the Default option or contact your monitor manufacturer to determine which monitor option you should select for your monitor to emulate.

3 For Gamma, type a value appropriate to your platform:

• On the Macintosh, type the value that you selected for Target Gamma in the Gamma control panel (see page 44). If you are using a third-party utility, enter the gamma value set by that device.

• In Windows, you should have already entered a value here. If not, go back to "Step 1: Calibrate your monitor" on page 43.

4 For White Point, select a setting.

If you are using a third-party monitor calibration device, choose the white point value established by that device; otherwise, leave this value at the default value of 6500K. If you don't see the value you need, select Custom, and type in your own value.

Note: For Windows, if you choose your monitor, the white point and phosphors are adjusted accordingly.

5 For Phosphors, select a monitor type.

If the correct type is not in the drop-down list, choose Custom, and enter the red, green, and blue chromaticity coordinates as specified by your monitor manufacturer. This option accounts for the different red, green, and blue phosphors used by monitors to display color.

6 For Ambient Light, select a setting:

• Select High if your room lighting is brighter than the on-screen image. Because the High setting has no effect on RGB-to-CMYK conversion, you should also select High if you are using hardware monitor calibration that accounts for ambient lighting.

• Select Low if your room lighting is not as bright as the screen.

• Select Medium if your room and monitor light levels are about the same.

7 Click OK to exit the dialog box.

You have completed the first aspect of the calibration process, which is adjusting the gamma settings and entering information about your monitor in the Monitor Setup dialog box. In Lesson 13, "Creating Color Separations," you'll complete the process by entering information about the properties of the inks and paper stock used to output your images
to print.

Review

• Why is it necessary to calibrate your monitor?

• What is the ideal environment for calibrating your monitor?

• How does monitor calibration influence the way colors appear in your final images?

• If you use different paper stocks in your work, what can you do to retain the settings for each paper you use?

4

Lesson 4

Working with Selections

Learning how to select areas of an image is of primary importance when working with Adobe Photoshop—you must first select what you want to affect. Once you've made a selection, only the area within a selection can be edited; areas outside the selection are protected from change. The Adobe Photoshop selection tools let you select by size, shape, and color.

In this lesson, you'll learn how to do the following:

• Use the selection tools and commands to select parts of an image in various ways.

• Move, rotate, scale, and duplicate selections.

• Crop an image.

Restoring default preferences

Before starting this lesson, delete the Adobe Photoshop Preferences file to restore the program's default palettes and command settings. If you need step-by-step instructions about how to delete the preferences file, see "Restoring default preferences" on page 4.

Restart Adobe Photoshop.

Getting started

Before you begin working, you'll open the finished art file to get an idea of what you'll create.

1 Choose File > Open. Locate and open the Lesson04 folder; then select End04.psd and click Open.

An image of a face, constructed using various types of vegetables, is displayed.

2 If desired, choose View > Zoom Out to make the image smaller and leave it on your screen as you work. If you don't want to leave the image open, choose File > Close.

Now, you'll open the start file and use selection tools and commands to combine the individual vegetables to construct a face. As you experiment with the selection tools, you'll learn which tools work best for specific types of selections.

3 Choose File > Open. Locate and open the Lesson04 folder, then select Start04.psd from the list of files and click Open.

4 Choose File > Save As, enter the name Work04.psd, and click Save.

Using the selection tools

There are four basic selection tools in the toolbox.

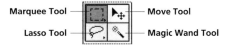

Marquee Tool — Move Tool
Lasso Tool — Magic Wand Tool

The marquee tool and the lasso tool contain hidden tools, which can be selected by holding down the mouse button and dragging to the desired tool in the menu.

The *marquee tool* lets you select rectangular or elliptical areas in an image.

The *lasso tool* lets you draw a freehand outline around an area. The *polygon lasso tool* lets you draw freehand straight lines around an area.

The *magic wand tool* lets you select parts of an image based on the color similarities of adjacent pixels. This tool is useful for selecting odd-shaped areas without having to trace a complex outline using the lasso tool.

The *move tool* lets you move a selection marquee or objects on a single layer.

Adobe Photoshop also includes a fifth selection tool—the *pen tool*, also located in the toolbox. You can use the pen tool to draw precise straight and curved lines, which can then be converted into selections. You'll learn how to use the pen tool in Lesson 9, "Basic Pen Tool Techniques."

Using tool options

Each tool has its own Options palette. To open the Options palette for a tool, you double-click the tool in the toolbox. The Options palette for the specific tool moves to the front of the Info/Navigator/Options palette group.

Creating a rectangular selection

You'll start by selecting the melon using the rectangle marquee tool.

1 Double-click the rectangle marquee tool (⬚) in the toolbox. The tool is selected and the Marquee Options palette appears.

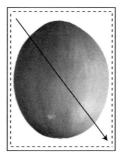

2 Drag the rectangle marquee tool diagonally down from the top left corner of the melon to the bottom right corner of the melon to create a selection marquee.

3 Click the move tool (⇖) in the toolbox (to the right of the rectangle marquee tool), and position the pointer within the selection. The pointer becomes an arrow with a pair of scissors, to indicate that dragging the selection will cut it from the present location and move it to the new location.

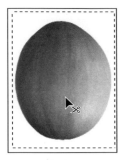

4 Drag the melon downward, toward the bottom of the window, leaving about an inch of blank space below the melon. Release the mouse button.

You can always undo your last action using the Undo command.

5 Choose Edit > Undo Move to undo the move; then choose Edit > Redo Move to move the melon back to the new location.

Before making your next selection, you'll deselect the current one. Use either of these methods to deselect an active selection:

• Choose Select > None.

• Click outside of the selection marquee anywhere in the window.

Creating an elliptical selection

The ellipse marquee tool lets you select elliptical or circular shapes. You'll use the ellipse marquee to select eyes for the face.

1 Click the zoom tool (🔍) in the toolbox and then click the zoom tool over the blueberry until you've zoomed in to a 200% view.

2 Select the ellipse marquee tool (⬭) from the toolbox in any of the following ways:

• Click and hold down the mouse button on the rectangle marquee tool to display the hidden tools, and then drag to the ellipse marquee tool and release the mouse button.

• Hold down the Option (Macintosh) or Alt (Windows) key and click the rectangle marquee tool. Each time you click while holding down the modifier key, the next hidden tool appears in the toolbox.

• Press *m*. *M* is the keyboard shortcut for both the elliptical and rectangle marquee tools. Pressing *m* repeatedly toggles between the two tools.

3 Move the pointer over the blueberry; the pointer becomes a crosshair.

4 Drag diagonally down from the top left edge of the blueberry to the lower right edge of the blueberry to create a selection marquee. *Do not* release the mouse button.

If a selection marquee isn't positioned exactly where you want it, you can adjust it while you drag the mouse to create it.

5 Still holding down the mouse button, hold down the Spacebar and drag; the selection marquee moves as you drag.

Before moving border   *After moving border*

6 Release the Spacebar and drag again. Notice that when you drag without the Spacebar, the size of the marquee changes, but the location of the marquee does not.

Dragging to resize selection border   *Result*

The Spacebar-drag method of moving a selection marquee while drawing works with any selection tool—just be sure to continue holding down the mouse button when you press the Spacebar and drag.

Take a moment to experiment with this method, and then use either method to perfect the selection around the blueberry.

In addition, you can move a selection marquee after you've released the mouse button.

7 Position the marquee tool anywhere inside the selection border surrounding the blueberry. The pointer becomes an arrow with a small selection icon next to it.

8 Drag to reposition the selection marquee around the blueberry.

Dragging within border to reposition marquee   *Result*

Any time an image contains an active selection, you can position the marquee tool, the lasso tool ($\wp$), or the magic wand tool ($\mathbf{\ast}\!\diagdown$) within the selection outline and drag to reposition the selection border.

Next you'll move the blueberry onto the carrot slice to create an eye for the face. At this point, you'll learn how to select the move tool using a keyboard shortcut. By holding down the Command (Macintosh) or Ctrl (Windows) key, you can select the move tool from the keyboard instead of selecting it from the toolbox (as you did in the first part of the lesson).

9 With the ellipse marquee tool still selected, hold down Command (Macintosh) or Ctrl (Windows), and position the pointer within the selection marquee.

A pair of scissors appears with the pointer, to indicate that the selection will be cut from its current location.

10 Drag the blueberry onto the carrot slice and release the mouse button and the Command/Ctrl key.

11 Choose Select > None to deselect everything.

12 Choose File > Save to save the artwork.

Softening the edges of selections

Anti-aliasing creates smooth edges around a selection by making the pixels that lie along the selection border partially transparent. The Anti-aliased option, available in the marquee, lasso, and magic wand options palettes, removes jagged edges, and is especially useful when you're building a composite image using selections from different parts of an image. See illustrations 4–1 and

4–2 in the color section of this book for samples of non-anti-aliased edges and anti-aliased edges.

You'll experiment with the anti-aliasing option using the carrot slice as a selection.

1 Double-click the ellipse marquee tool in the toolbox. (Although the elliptical tool is already selected from the last part of the lesson, double-clicking the tool brings the Marquee Options palette to the front.)

2 Notice that the Anti-aliased option is selected in the Marquee Options palette, indicating that any selection you make will be anti-aliased.

3 Drag an elliptical marquee around the carrot slice containing the blueberry. If necessary, adjust the selection marquee using one of the methods you learned earlier.

To see the effect of the Anti-aliased option, you must move the selection from its original location. In this case, you'll move and duplicate the selection simultaneously.

4 Click the move tool (⬥⊹) in the toolbox, then hold down Option (Macintosh) or Alt (Windows) and position the pointer within the selection. The pointer becomes a double arrow, which indicates that a duplicate will be made when you move the selection.

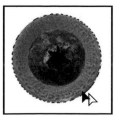

5 Continue holding down Option/Alt, and drag the selection into the *scratch area* (the gray area above the carrot slice). Release the mouse button, then release Option/Alt.

6 Choose Select > None to deselect everything.

7 Click the zoom tool and zoom in on the edges of the carrot slice.

Notice that the edges of the carrot slice appear to be smooth (anti-aliased). Next, you'll see how the edges of the carrot slice look when you turn off the Anti-aliased option.

8 Click the marquee tool in the toolbox. In the Marquee Options palette, click the Anti-aliased option to turn it off.

9 Drag a marquee around the original carrot slice to select it again. If necessary, adjust the selection marquee using one of the methods you learned earlier.

10 Click the move tool (✛) in the toolbox, hold down Option (Macintosh) or Alt (Windows), and position the pointer within the selection, and then drag another copy of the carrot onto the Scratch Area, next to the anti-aliased carrot slice.

11 Choose Select > None to deselect everything.

12 Click the zoom tool; then zoom in on the edges of the carrot to see the edges.

The first selection, with the anti-aliased option turned on, has smooth edges; the second selection, with the anti-aliased

option turn off, has jagged edges. In general, it's a good idea to leave anti-aliasing turned on when you're selecting and moving parts of an image.

13 Choose File > Save to save your work.

Next, you'll learn about softening the edges of a selection using the feathering option. *Feathering* a selection blurs the edges of a selection when you cut, copy, move, or fill the selection. Feathering works by creating a gradual transition from the hard edges of the selection into the pixels in the surrounding area. For a sample of a feathered edge, see illustration 4–3 in the color section of this book.

To see how feathered edges differ from anti-aliased edges and jagged edges, you'll apply a feather radius to the carrot slice and move it into the scratch area.

14 Click the ellipse marquee tool in the toolbox. In the Marquee Options palette, enter a value of 3 in the Feather text box.

15 Again, drag an elliptical marquee around the carrot slice containing the blueberry.

16 Click the move tool (✛) in the toolbox, hold down Option (Macintosh) or Alt (Windows), and then drag the selection to the scratch area.

17 Choose Select > None to deselect everything.

Notice that feathering affects both the inside and outside edges of a selection, and anti-aliasing affects only the outside edges of a selection.

Now that you've practiced setting different options for the edges of selections, you'll select and duplicate the carrot slice eye onto the melon face.

18 Choose View > Fit on Screen to resize the document to fit on your screen.

19 Using the ellipse marquee tool, select the edge option you like best, and then select the original carrot-blueberry eye.

20 Click the move tool (✛) in the toolbox, hold down Option (Macintosh) or Alt (Windows), and then drag a duplicate of the eye onto the melon face. Do not deselect.

21 To create a second eye, hold down Option/Alt, and drag to create a duplicate of the eye.

22 Choose Layer > Transform > Flip Horizontal to adjust the eye for the right side of the face.

23 Choose Select > None to deselect everything; then choose File > Save to save your work.

Selecting from a center point

Sometimes it's easier to make elliptical or rectangular selections by drawing a selection marquee from the center point of the object to the outside edge.

You'll select the kiwi fruit to create a mouth for the face.

1 Position the ellipse marquee tool at the approximate center of the kiwi; then hold down Option (Macintosh) or Alt

(Windows) and drag. The selection is created from the center point to the outside edge.

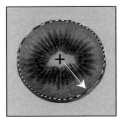

You can use a keyboard shortcut to move and duplicate a selection simultaneously.

2 Position the ellipse marquee tool within the selection, then hold down Command+Option (Macintosh) or Ctrl+Alt (Windows), and drag to move a copy of the kiwi mouth onto the face. Release the mouse button; then release the modifier keys.

3 Choose Select > None to deselect everything.

4 Choose File > Save to save the artwork.

Selecting with the magic wand tool

The magic wand tool lets you select adjacent pixels in an image based on their similarity in color. You'll use the magic wand tool to select the pear tomato, which you'll use as a nose for the face.

1 Double-click the magic wand (✎) tool in the toolbox to select the tool and its options palette.

In the Magic Wand Options palette, the Tolerance setting controls how many similar tones of a color are selected when you click an area. The default value is 32, indicating that 32 similar lighter tones and 32 similar darker tones will be selected.

2 For Tolerance, enter 48 to increase the number of shades that will be selected when you click the magic wand.

3 Click the magic wand tool anywhere within the pear tomato. Most of it will be selected.

4 To select the remaining areas of the pear tomato, hold down the Shift key and click the unselected areas.

You'll notice that when you hold down the Shift key, a plus sign appears with the magic wand (✎) pointer, to indicate that you're adding to the current selection.

5 When the pear tomato is completely selected, hold down Command+Option (Macintosh) or Ctrl+Alt (Windows), position the pointer within the selection, and drag the tomato nose on the melon face. *Do not deselect.*

6 Choose File > Save to save your work.

Adjusting a selection

You can make minor adjustments to the position of a selection using the arrow keys. The arrow keys let you nudge a selection one pixel at a time or five pixels at a time.

1 Press the up (⬆) arrow key a few times to move the nose upward. Notice that each time you press the arrow key, the nose moves in 1-pixel increments. Experiment with the other arrow keys to see how they affect the selection.

2 Next, hold down Shift and press an arrow key. Notice that the selection moves in 5-pixel increments.

Sometimes, the selection marquee around an area can distract you as you make adjustments. You can hide the edges of a selection temporarily without actually deselecting, and then display the selection marquee once you've completed the adjustments.

3 Choose View > Hide Edges. The selection marquee around the pear tomato disappears.

4 Use the arrow keys again to nudge the pear tomato nose. When the nose is positioned where you want it, choose View > Show Edges.

5 Choose Select > None to deselect everything.

6 Choose File > Save to save the artwork.

Adding to and subtracting from a selection

You can start a selection by drawing a rough outline around the desired area, and then refine it using the selection tools to add to and subtract from the selection.

You'll make a rough selection of the grapefruit using the lasso tool and then use selection options to perfect it. The grapefruit selection will become the melon face's ear!

1 Double-click the lasso tool (◯) in the toolbox to select the tool and open its options palette.

2 Drag a rough outline to create an ear shape around the grapefruit (include some of the white area outside the pink fruit).

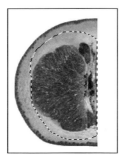

3 You'll begin by adding to the current selection. Locate a part of the selection marquee within the pink section of the grapefruit.

4 With the lasso tool selected, hold down Shift. A plus sign appears with the lasso tool pointer, to indicate that you'll add to the selection.

5 Drag the lasso tool around the area you want to add to the selection; then release the mouse button. The area is added to the current selection.

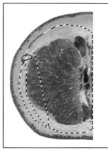 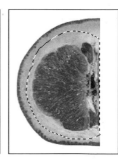

Shift-drag to add to the selection   *Result*

Note: *If you release the mouse button while drawing a marquee, the selection closes itself by drawing a straight line between the starting point and the point where you release the mouse. To create a precise selection, it's a good idea to end the selection by crossing the starting point.*

Next, you'll remove, or subtract, part of the selection. Locate a part of the selection marquee that is in the white area of the grapefruit (or has extended into the gray area), outside the pink section.

6 Hold down Option (Macintosh) or Alt (Windows). A minus sign appears with the lasso tool pointer.

7 Drag the lasso tool around a small area you want to remove from the selection; then repeat the process until you've finished removing all the unwanted parts of the selection.

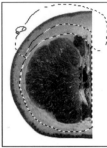 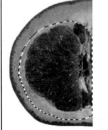

Option/Alt-drag to subtract from the selection   *Result*

💡 When adding to or subtracting from a selection using the lasso tool, it's a good idea to work in small sections to maintain greater control over the selection.

8 To duplicate and move the ear onto the melon face, hold down Command+Option (Macintosh) or Ctrl+Alt (Windows), and drag a copy of the ear to the left side of the face. *Do not deselect.*

9 Choose File > Save to save your work.

Scaling and rotating a selection

The Free Transform command lets you scale and rotate a selection in one operation. You'll scale and rotate the first ear, and then duplicate and flip a copy to create a second ear.

1 Choose Layer > Free Transform. The transformation boundary appears around the ear selection.

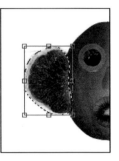

2 To scale the ear, position the pointer directly on one of the corner handles and drag to reduce the size of the ear. If desired, hold down the Shift key as you drag a corner handle to scale the ear proportionately.

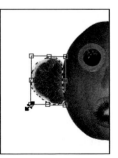

3 If desired, you can reposition the ear by dragging anywhere within the transformation boundary.

4 To rotate the ear, position the pointer outside a corner handle until you see a double-headed arrow, and then drag to rotate the ear.

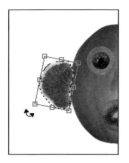

5 Press Return to apply the transformation. The ear remains selected.

6 Position the pointer within the selection; then hold down Command+Option+Shift (Macintosh) or Ctrl+Alt+Shift (Windows), and drag to duplicate and reposition the ear on the right side of the face. Holding down Shift as you drag constrains the movement of the ear horizontally.

7 Choose Layer > Transform > Flip Horizontal to adjust the ear for the right side of the face.

8 If desired, position the pointer within the selection and drag to reposition it at the right side of the melon face.

9 If necessary, choose Layer > Free Transform; then rotate the ear to fit the right side of the face.

10 Press Return (Macintosh) or Enter (Windows) to complete the transformation.

11 Choose Select > None to deselect everything; then choose File > Save to save the artwork.

Drawing freehand and straight line selections

You can use the lasso tool to make selections that require both freehand and straight lines. You'll select a bow tie for the face using the lasso tool this way. It takes a bit of practice to use the lasso tool to alternate between straight line and freehand selections—if you make a mistake while you're selecting the bow tie, simply deselect and start again.

1 Click the zoom tool in the toolbox. Then click twice on the bow tie pasta to enlarge its view.

2 Double-click the lasso tool ($\wp$) in the toolbox to select the tool and open its Options palette.

3 Starting at the top left corner of the bow tie pasta, drag to the right to create a freehand outline across the curves at the top of the bow tie. (Again, don't worry about making a perfect selection.) Continue holding down the mouse.

4 To select the right edge of the bow tie, hold down Option (Macintosh) or Alt (Windows), and click the mouse button along the right edge of the bow tie to draw straight lines. Do not release the mouse button when you've finished.

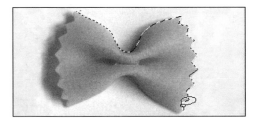

5 Release Option/Alt, and drag to the left to create a freehand outline across the bottom of the bow tie.

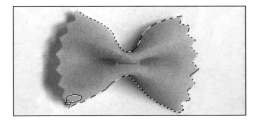

6 To complete the selection outline, hold down Option/Alt again, and click the mouse button along the left edge of the bow tie to draw straight lines.

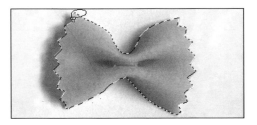

7 To complete the selection marquee, make sure the last straight line crosses the start of the selection, release the Option/Alt, and then release the mouse button.

Important: *To complete a selection using the lasso tool, end the outline by crossing the starting point.*

8 Before you move the bow tie into position, double-click the hand tool in the toolbox to fit the entire image in the window.

9 Select the move tool from the toolbox; then hold down Option (Macintosh) or Alt (Windows), and drag the bow tie selection to make a copy at the bottom of the melon face.

10 If you want to change the size of the bow tie, choose Layer > Free Transform and scale the bow tie before continuing.

11 Choose File > Save to save the artwork.

Combining selection tools

You may find that using more than one selection tool works well to select certain shapes or objects. You'll use both the magic wand tool and the ellipse marquee tool to select the squash flower for the bow tie.

1 Select the magic wand tool (⬙) in the toolbox.

2 Click anywhere in the yellow area of the squash. Most of the squash is selected, with the exception of the stem in the center.

3 Click the ellipse marquee tool in the toolbox; then hold down the Shift key and position the pointer within the squash selection. Notice that a plus sign appears with the crosshair.

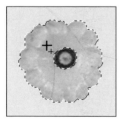

4 Drag a marquee around the stem at the center of the squash, release the mouse button, and then release Shift.

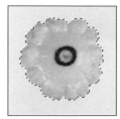

5 Hold down Command+Option (Macintosh) or Ctrl+Alt (Windows), and drag the squash onto the bow tie.

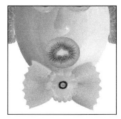

As you already know, the magic wand tool makes selections based on color. If an object you want to select is on a solid-colored background, it can be much easier to select the background color with the magic wand tool and then reverse the selection to select the desired area or object.

You'll see how this works by using the rectangle marquee tool and the magic wand tool to select radish eyebrows for the face.

6 Select the rectangle marquee tool (▢) from the hidden tools under the ellipse marquee tool in the toolbox.

7 In the Marquee Options palette, enter a value of 0 in the Feather text box. (It's still selected from earlier in the lesson.)

8 Hold down Command+Spacebar (Macintosh) or Ctrl+Spacebar (Windows) to select the zoom-in tool from the keyboard, and then click over the radishes to magnify the view.

9 Drag a rectangular marquee around the radishes. Include the white background in the selection, but don't include any of the gray from the surrounding areas.

At this point, the radishes and the white background area are selected. You'll subtract the white area from the selection, resulting in only the radishes being selected.

10 Click the magic wand tool in the toolbox; then hold down Option (Macintosh) or Alt (Windows). A minus sign appears with the magic wand pointer.

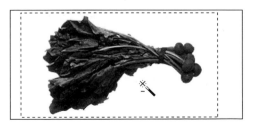

11 Click anywhere in the white area surrounding the radishes. Now only the radishes are selected!

To reduce the view of the image in the window, you'll zoom out using a similar method to the one you used to zoom in on the radishes.

12 Hold down Spacebar+Option (Macintosh) or Spacebar+Alt (Windows). Notice that the pointer becomes the zoom-out tool.

13 Click once over the radishes to reduce the view of the image in the window; then release Spacebar+Option/Alt.

Press Spacebar+Option (Macintosh) or Spacebar+Alt (Windows) to select the zoom-out tool without deselecting the currently active tool.

14 To duplicate and move the radish eyebrow to the melon face, hold down Command+Option (Macintosh) or

Ctrl+Alt (Windows) and drag the radish above the left eye on the melon face. Do not deselect.

15 Hold down Command+Option/ Ctrl+Alt, position the pointer within the selection, and drag to duplicate and reposition another eyebrow above the right eye.

16 Choose Layer > Transform > Flip Horizontal to adjust the right eyebrow. If desired, reposition the eyebrow using any of the methods you learned.

17 Choose Select > None to deselect everything.

18 Choose File > Save to save your work.

Your fruit-and-vegetable face is almost complete. You'll add a mushroom hat to the melon face and then add some detail to the hat to complete the lesson.

19 Click the lasso tool in the toolbox; then select the mushroom by drawing a freehand outline around it.

20 Hold down Command+Option/ Ctrl+Alt, position the pointer within the selection, and then drag the mushroom hat onto the melon face.

21 Choose Select > None to deselect everything.

Selecting with the Color Range command

The Color Range command lets you select a color within a selection or within an entire image. You can select specific colors in an image, such as all the greens or blues, or you can select a color from the image using the eyedropper tool within the Color Range dialog box.

You'll use the Color Range command to select the purple peas for the decoration on the mushroom hat.

1 Hold down Command+Spacebar (Macintosh) or Ctrl+Spacebar (Windows) to select the zoom tool from the keyboard; then click over the peas to magnify the view.

2 Select the rectangle marquee tool in the toolbox; then drag a rectangular marquee around the gray area that borders the peas.

When using the Color Range command, you don't have to make a selection first—in this case, selecting the area first lets you isolate the part of the image you want to select.

3 Choose Select > Color Range.

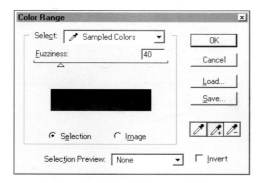

At the top of the Color Range dialog box, the default selection type is Sampled Colors. Sampled colors are the colors you take a *sample* of by clicking the eyedropper on a part of the image.

Below the image preview area of the dialog box, the Selection option is turned on and the preview area is black. The black area of the preview indicates that none of the image is selected. Three eyedroppers at the right side of the dialog box let you control how many colors you want to select in the image. The first eyedropper selects a single color;

the eyedropper with a plus sign adds colors to a current selection; and the eyedropper with a minus sign subtracts colors from a current selection.

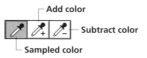

To add to or subtract from a selection, you can either click the appropriate eyedropper or you can drag the eyedropper through an area to select a range of colors.

To select the peas, you'll use the eyedropper-plus tool and drag through a pea in the image window to select all the colors in the peas.

4 Click the eyedropper-plus tool (🖊) in the Color Range dialog box; then position the pointer in the image window and drag through one of the peas.

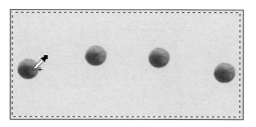

As you drag, notice that the peas in the preview area of the Color Range dialog box turn white, indicating that they're selected.

If you make a mistake and select part of the gray area as well as the peas, click the eyedropper-minus tool, and click or drag on the areas you don't want selected.

5 When the peas are completely white, click OK. The peas are selected in the image window.

6 Choose View > Fit on Screen to fit the entire image to your screen; then hold down Command+Option (Macintosh) or Ctrl+Alt (Windows), position the pointer within the selection, and drag to duplicate and reposition a copy of the peas on the mushroom hat.

7 Choose File > Save to save your work.

Cropping the completed image

To complete the artwork, you'll crop the image to a final size.

1 Choose the crop tool (⛏) from the toolbox. The crop tool is located in the hidden tools palette under the marquee tool.

Move the pointer into the image window and drag diagonally from the top left corner to the bottom right corner of the completed artwork to create a crop marquee.

2 If you need to reposition the crop marquee, position the pointer anywhere inside the marquee and drag.

3 If you want to resize the marquee, drag a handle.

4 Choose File > Save to save your completed artwork.

When the marquee is positioned where you want it, press Return to crop the image. The fruit-and-vegetable face is complete.

Review

• Once you've made a selection, what area of the selection can be edited?

• How can you add to or subtract from a selection?

• How can you move a selection marquee while you're drawing it?

• When creating selections with the lasso tool, what can you do to ensure that the selection starts and ends where you want it to?

• How does the magic wand tool determine which areas of an image to select? What is Tolerance, and how does it affect a selection?

• How does the Color Range command differ from the magic wand tool?

• What are the different types of edges a selection can have, and which one would you choose when building a composite image from various selections?

• When is it useful to combine selection tools?

5

Lesson 5

Layer Basics

Adobe Photoshop lets you isolate different parts of an image on layers. The artwork on each layer can be edited as a discrete image, allowing for unlimited flexibility in editing.

In this lesson, you'll learn how to do the following:

• Organize your artwork on layers.

• View and hide layers.

• Select layers.

• View the transparent area of a layer.

• Reorder layers to change the placement of artwork in the image.

• Create a new layer.

• Apply modes to layers to vary the effect of artwork on the layer.

• Move layers from one file to another.

• Erase objects on layers and delete layers.

• Link layers in order to affect them simultaneously.

• Merge like layers to reduce the size of a file.

• Save a layered file.

Restoring default preferences

Before starting this lesson, delete the Adobe Photoshop Preferences file to restore the program's default palettes and command settings. If you need step-by-step instructions about how to delete the preferences file, see "Restoring default preferences" on page 4.

Restart Adobe Photoshop.

Getting started

Before you begin working, you'll open the finished art file and look at the completed image to get an idea of what you'll create.

1 Choose File > Open. Locate and open the Lesson05 folder, then select End05.psd and click Open.

An image of a figure on a beach is displayed.

2 If desired, choose View > Zoom Out to make the image smaller and leave it on your screen as you work. If you don't want to leave the image open, choose File > Close.

Now, you'll open the start file and work with the image as you learn about the Layers palette and layer options.

3 Choose File > Open. Locate and open the Lesson05 folder, then select Start05.psd from the list of files and click Open.

4 Choose File > Save As, enter the name Work05.psd, and click Save.

Organizing artwork on layers

Every Adobe Photoshop image contains one or more *layers*. Every new file is created with a *background*, which can be converted to a layer. When you scan an image and open it in Adobe Photoshop, it is placed on the background.

Layers in Adobe Photoshop are analogous to placing portions of a drawing on sheets of acetate—when the sheets are stacked, the entire drawing is visible, but individual sheets of acetate may be edited, repositioned, or deleted without affecting the overall drawing.

In Adobe Photoshop, the order in which the layers of a drawing are organized is called the *stacking order.* The stacking order of layers determines how the image is viewed— you can change the layer order to make certain parts of the image appear in front of or behind other layers.

Viewing a layered document

All layers in an image are transparent until you add artwork (pixel values) to the layer. After you've added artwork to a layer, the areas that remain transparent are represented by a checkerboard.

Using the Layers palette

The Layers palette lets you control the layers in your document. You can create new layers, reposition layers, delete or merge layers, and apply effects, called *modes,* to individual layers.

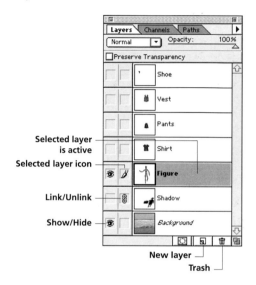

1 If the Layers palette is not visible on your screen, choose Window > Show Layers.

2 If necessary, click the Layers tab to bring the Layers palette to the front of its palette group.

3 Click the size box (Macintosh) or the Maximize box (Windows) in the top right area of the Layers palette to expand to the full size of the palette. (The palette size depends on the number of layers in the document.)

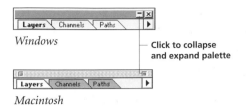

Windows

Click to collapse and expand palette

Macintosh

The Layers palette displays the layers in the active window from top to bottom. A thumbnail of the layer appears to the left of the layer name and is automatically updated as you edit the layer.

Viewing and hiding layers

The eye icon in the column to the left of the layer names indicates that a layer is visible. You can view or hide one or more layers by clicking the eye icon next to the layer name you want to view or hide. You can also drag through the eye column to turn multiple layers on or off.

1 Drag through the eye column from the top to the bottom to turn on all the layers in the image.

2 Drag through the eye column again from the top to the bottom to turn off all the layers in the image. The entire image disappears because all the layers are hidden.

The checkerboard indicates that with all the layers hidden, the image area is transparent.

3 Try showing and hiding different combinations of layers by clicking, or by clicking and dragging the eye column next to various layers.

4 Drag through the eye column from the top to the bottom to turn on all the layers in the image.

You can also hide all but a single layer.

5 To hide all but a single layer, Option-click (Macintosh) or Alt-click (Windows) the eye icon to the left of the layer you want to display. All the layers except the layer you clicked are hidden.

6 To display all the layers, Option-click (Macintosh) or Alt-click (Windows) the same layer again.

Selecting layers

You can select and edit a single layer at a time. The selected layer is called the *active layer*. When a layer is active, a paintbrush icon appears to the left of the layer name next to the eye column.

1 In the Layers palette, click the Vest layer (on the name or on the thumbnail) to make it the active layer.

Notice that the name of the active layer appears in the title bar of the image window.

2 Drag the Opacity slider triangle in the Layers palette to about 50%.

The Vest layer becomes 50% opaque and you can see the shirt and the pants underneath. The change affects only the artwork on the Vest layer.

3 Drag the Opacity slider back to 100%.

4 Click the eye icon next to the Vest layer to turn off the layer.

Next, you'll rearrange layers to change the order in which they appear.

Rearranging layers

You can rearrange layers to change the stacking order of the elements on individual layers. You'll rearrange the shirt layer to move it in front of the Pants layer.

1 Click the Shirt layer in the Layers palette to select it, and then drag upward to position it above the Pants layer. When you see a thick black line above the Pants layer, release the mouse button. The Shirt layer moves in front of the Pants layer.

Repositioning layer   *Result*

Renaming layers

You can change the name of a layer using the Layer Options dialog box.

1 In the Layers palette, double-click the Pants layer.

2 In the Layer Options dialog box, enter the name **Shorts** and click OK.

3 Choose File > Save to save your work.

Editing the background

By default, the *background* in an image cannot be moved and always appears in italic type at the bottom of the Layers palette. If you try to move the background, an icon appears to indicate that it can't be moved. If you want to move the background or change its opacity, you must first convert it to a layer by renaming it.

1 In the Layers palette, double-click the background to open the Make Layer dialog box.

2 Type the name **Seascape** and click OK. The background is renamed and can be edited as any other layer in the file.

3 In the Layers palette, drag the Opacity slider to about 60% to make the Seascape layer semitransparent.

Changing the view of the transparent areas in an image

At the beginning of this lesson, you learned that the transparent areas on a layer or in an image are represented by a checkerboard. You can modify the color and size of the checkerboard, or you can make the checkerboard invisible.

1 In the Layers palette, Option-click (Macintosh) or Alt-click (Windows) the eye icon next to the Figure layer to turn off all the layers except the Figure layer.

The area surrounding the figure is transparent, as indicated by the checkerboard.

2 Choose File > Preferences > Transparency & Gamut.

Checkerboard indicating transparency

3 For Grid Size, choose Small to change the size of the squares in the checkerboard.

4 For Grid Colors, choose one of the pre-defined colors to change the color of the checkerboard.

5 Experiment with various checkerboard sizes and colors.

6 Before closing the Transparency & Gamut dialog box, choose None for Grid Size to turn off the grid.

Note: When you choose None for the Checker-board option, the white area surrounding the artwork on a layer represents the transparent area.

7 Click OK.

8 In the Layers palette, Option-click (Macintosh) or Alt-click (Windows) the eye icon next to the Figure layer to turn on all the layers in the image.

Adding a new layer

Next, you'll create a new layer and add a gradient to it.

1 In the Layers palette, click the Seascape layer to make it the active layer.

2 Choose New Layer from the Layers palette menu.

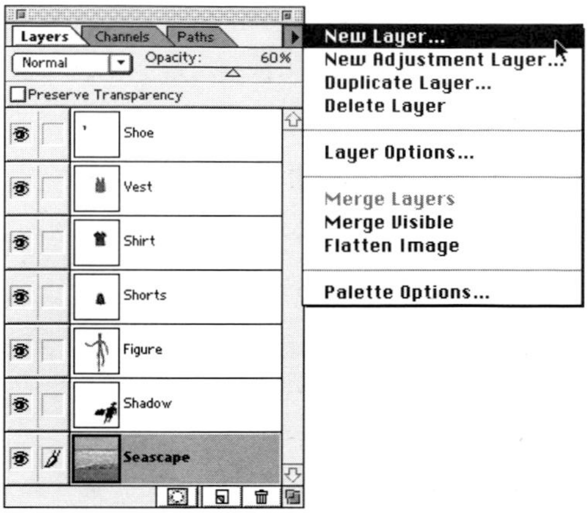

3 In the New Layer dialog box, type the name **Gradient** and click OK. The Gradient layer appears above the Seascape layer in the Layers palette.

4 Click the size box (Macintosh) or the Maximize box (Windows) in the Layers palette to display the full size of the Layers palette.

Adding a gradient to a layer

A gradient is a gradual blend from one color to another. The transition from one color to another may be subtle or sharp, which can be controlled using the gradient tool. You'll apply a gradient to the layer above the Seascape layer.

1 Double-click the gradient tool (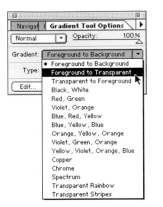) in the toolbox to select the tool and to open its Options palette.

2 In the Gradient Tool Options palette, for Gradient choose the Foreground to Transparent option.

6 In the image window, drag the gradient tool from the top of the image to the bottom of the image.

The gradient is applied over the length of the layer, starting with purple and gradually blending to transparent.

3 Click the Swatches palette tab to bring it to the front of its palette group. You'll select a shade of purple for the starting color of the gradient.

4 In the Swatches palette, click a shade of purple that appeals to you.

5 Make sure that the Gradient layer is the selected layer in the Layers palette.

7 In the Layers palette, drag the Opacity slider to 60% to lighten the gradient.

1 With the Gradient layer still the active layer, choose Darken from the mode menu (to the left of the Opacity slider in the Layers palette).

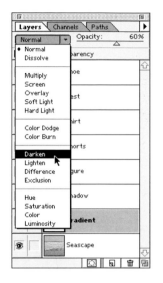

Note: If you are working on a 256-color monitor, you may see banding in the gradient.

Applying modes to a layer

Blending modes let you change the effect of artwork on a layer. For example, if you want to add color to a grayscale image to create a hand-painted look, you would select a mode. Layer modes let you change the effect of the artwork on an entire layer. You'll experiment with a few modes on the Gradient layer to see how the gradient is affected.

The Darken mode applies the colors in the gradient to only the pixels on the Seascape layer that are lighter than the gradient colors.

2 Next, choose Lighten from the mode menu.

The Lighten mode applies the colors in the gradient to only the pixels on the Seascape layer that are darker than the gradient colors.

3 Experiment by selecting other modes to apply a variety of effects to the Gradient layer.

For a sample of the effect of each layer mode, see illustration 5–1 in the color section of this book.

For a complete explanation of each layer mode, see the *Adobe Photoshop User Guide*.

4 Choose File > Save to save your work.

Moving layers between files

You can drag and drop layers from one file into another. You'll drag a layer containing three hats from one file into the Work05.psd file.

1 Choose File > Open, locate the Lesson05 folder, then select the Hats.psd file from the list and click Open. An image of three hats appears, and a single layer named Three Hats is displayed in the Layers palette.

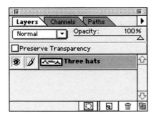

You'll drag and drop the Three Hats layer from the Hats file into the Work05.psd file.

2 Position the pointer on the Three Hats layer in the Layers palette, and then drag the layer onto the Work05.psd window. Release the mouse button when an outline appears in the Work05.psd image.

3 Notice that the Three Hats layer now appears in the Work05.psd Layers palette. When you dragged, the layer was duplicated and added to the Layers palette.

4 Drag the Three Hats layer to the top of the Layers palette to position it at the top level of the image.

5 Close the Hats file and do not save changes, if prompted.

Moving selections on layers

You can use the move tool to reposition the artwork on individual layers.

1 Click the move tool (⊹) in the toolbox.

2 In the Layers palette, make sure that the Three Hats layer is the active layer.

3 Decide which hat you want to place on the figure's head. Then with the move tool, drag the hat into position. (Don't worry about the other two hats just yet.)

Erasing artwork on a layer

You can erase parts of a layer or an entire layer. You'll use the eraser tool to edit the image a few different ways.

1 Double-click the eraser tool (✐) in the toolbox. The Eraser Options palette appears.

2 Choose Block from the Erase Options menu; then move the eraser tool into the window. The eraser becomes a square block.

3 With the Three Hats layer still selected, drag the eraser over the hats you didn't select.

4 In the Layers palette, click the Figure layer to make it active.

5 In the Eraser Options palette, select the Paintbrush option, set the Opacity to 65%, and then drag the eraser tool over the figure's right leg to immerse it in the water.

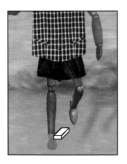

Deleting a layer

You can delete unwanted or unused layers from an image.

Delete the Shoe layer in either of the following ways:

• Make sure that the Shoe layer is the active layer, and then choose Delete Layer from the Layers palette menu.

• Drag the Shoe layer in the Layers palette onto the Trash button at the bottom of the Layers palette.

Scaling and rotating objects

You can scale and rotate a selection simultaneously using the Free Transform command. You'll scale and rotate a basket for the figure.

1 Choose File > Open, locate the Lesson05 folder and select the Basket.psd file; then click Open.

2 In the Layers palette, position the pointer on the Basket layer and then drag the layer into the Work05.psd file. Release the mouse button when an outline appears in the Work05.psd window.

3 Close the Basket image and do not save changes, if prompted.

4 Click the move tool in the toolbox, and then drag the basket into position on the figure's right arm.

5 Choose Layer > Free Transform. The transformation boundary appears around the basket.

6 Rotate the basket by positioning the pointer outside one of the handles and dragging.

Position pointer outside handles. . .   *and drag to rotate an object.*

7 Scale the basket to a smaller size by holding down the Shift key and dragging a handle of the transformation boundary.

8 If necessary, position the pointer inside the free transformation boundary and drag to reposition the basket.

9 Press Return to apply the transformation changes.

10 Double-click the eraser tool in the toolbox. In the Eraser Options palette, drag the Opacity slider to 100%; then erase a portion of the basket handle to fit it on the figure's arm.

Linking layers

You can link two or more layers in a document to affect them as a group. You'll link all of the layers except the background Seascape layer.

1 In the Layers palette, click the Basket layer to make it the active layer.

2 Next, click the small box to the right of the eye icon in each of the remaining layers, with the exception of the Gradient layer, the Shadow layer, and the Seascape layer.

When you click in this box, a link icon appears. (The active layer does not display a link icon, but it is part of the linked layers.)

3 Click the move tool in the toolbox, then position it in the image window and begin dragging. You'll notice that the figure, the clothing, and the accessories move simultaneously. Align the figure with the shadow to complete the image!

4 Unlink all the linked layers by clicking the link icon next to each linked layer.

How layers affect file size

Each layer you add to an image increases the file size. The amount that the file size increases is related to how much pixel information is on the layer—transparent areas of the layer do not add to the file size. To keep the file size manageable, it's a good idea to

merge layers you've finished working with and delete any unused layers in the image. However, don't merge or delete layers until you've made final design decisions.

Merging layers

You can merge all visible layers in a file, or you can merge all of the layers below the selected layer. You'll use the Merge Visible Layers command to merge only the visible layers in the image.

1 In the Layers palette, click the eye icon next to the Seascape layer, the Shadow layer, and the Gradient layer to hide them.

2 Choose Merge Visible from the Layers palette menu.

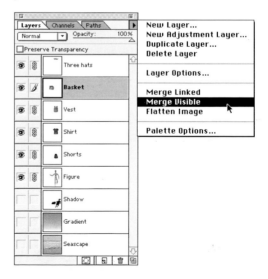

All of the layers are merged, with the exception of the Seascape, Shadow, and Gradient layers.

3 Drag through the column next to the Seascape, Shadow, and Gradient layers to make them visible before continuing.

Flattening files

When you have edited all the layers in your image, you use the Flatten Image command to merge all the layers in the image into a single background layer, thus greatly reducing the file size.

In most cases, you shouldn't flatten an image until you are absolutely certain that you have finished all of your design decisions.

1 From the Layers palette menu, choose Flatten Image. All the layers in the Work05.psd image are merged onto a single background.

2 Choose File > Save As, enter the name Flat05.psd, and click Save.

3 To see the difference in the size of the two files, choose File > Open, locate the Lesson05 folder, then select each of the files in the file list (Work05.psd and Flat05.psd). When you select a file in a list of files, its size is displayed at the bottom of the Open dialog box.

You've completed the Layer Basics lesson. Later, in Lesson 8, "Advanced Layer Techniques," you'll learn advanced layer concepts.

Review

• What is the advantage of using layers?

• How can you make artwork on one layer appear in front of artwork on another layer?

• How can you move a layer from one image into another image?

• How can you adjust multiple layers simultaneously?

• When you've completed your artwork, what can you do to a file to minimize its size?

6

Lesson 6

Painting and Editing

The Adobe Photoshop painting tools let you create original artwork or retouch existing artwork. You can apply paint at various opacity levels, creating a transparent effect, and you can select from several different types of painting tools.

In this lesson, you'll learn how to do the following:

• Use the painting tools to create original artwork and to apply a variety of painting effects to existing artwork.

• Understand the relationship between a painting tool, its Options palette, and its brush size.

• Select paint colors from the Color palette, the Swatches palette, and the Adobe Photoshop Color Picker.

• Select options for the painting tools to enhance the behavior of the tools.

Restoring default preferences

Before starting this lesson, delete the Adobe Photoshop Preferences file to restore the program's default palettes and command settings. If you need step-by-step instructions about how to delete the preferences file, see "Restoring default preferences" on page 4.

Restart Adobe Photoshop.

Getting started

Before you begin working, you'll open the finished art to get an idea of what you'll create.

1 Choose File > Open. Locate and open the Lesson06 folder, then select End06.psd and click Open.

2 If desired, choose View > Zoom Out to make the image smaller and leave it on your screen as you work. If you don't want to leave the image open, choose File > Close.

You'll begin by opening a black-and-white line drawing of the coyote, and then you'll color the drawing using a variety of painting tools and options.

3 Choose File > Open. Locate and open the Lesson06 folder, then select Start06.psd and click Open.

4 Choose File > Save As, enter the name Work06.psd, and click Save.

As you work with the painting tools to complete the drawing, don't worry about selecting the "right" colors or creating an exact replica of the drawing. The purpose of the lesson is to help you become familiar with the various painting tools to create a piece of artwork that reflects your personal preferences.

Using the painting tools

In general, the airbrush tool, the paintbrush tool, the line tool, the pencil tool, and the rubber stamp tool are referred to as the painting tools. Sometimes the paint bucket tool, the eyedropper tool, the eraser tool, and the gradient tool are also included in this category.

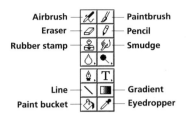

Tools, tool size, and tool options

By default, each painting tool is of a certain size and paints at a particular opacity. The default size of a painting tool is displayed in the Brushes palette; the default opacity of a tool is displayed in its corresponding Options palette. It's very important to understand the relationship between a tool, its brush size, and its Options palette, because they have a cumulative effect when you paint.

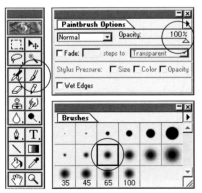

Selected tool, its Options palette, and current brush size

1 Double-click the paintbrush tool (✏) in the toolbox.

Notice that the default opacity setting in the Paintbrush Options palette is 100%.

2 Now, click the Brushes palette tab to bring the palette to the front of its group. The default brush size for the paintbrush tool is highlighted.

Displaying painting tools

Each tool has a *hot spot*, the point from which the tool's action begins. By default, when you select a tool and move it into the image window, the pointer becomes an icon of the tool in the toolbox.

For painting tools, it's helpful to change the way they're displayed so you can see the actual size of the painting tool in pixels.

1 Choose File > Preferences > General to open the Preferences dialog box.

The Preferences dialog box contains several groups of settings that apply to various aspects of the program. You can select a group of settings from the menu at the top of the dialog box, or you can click the Next and Prev buttons to move through the settings.

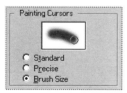

2 Click the Next button twice to get to the Display & Cursors section of the Preferences dialog box.

3 In the Painting Cursors section of the dialog box, click Brush Size.

4 Click OK.

5 Position the paintbrush tool in the window again; the pointer displays the paintbrush by its size in pixels.

Changing brush opacity

The transparency of brush strokes is determined by the Opacity level set in the Paintbrush Options palette. The lower the value you set, the more transparent the paint.

1 Click the Paintbrush Options tab to bring the palette to the front of its group.

2 Change the opacity level of paint in either of the following ways:

• By dragging the Opacity slider in the painting tool's Options palette.

Opacity slider

• By typing a number on your keypad. If you type a number from 1 to 10, the opacity changes in 10% increments. (If you want to set the opacity to an increment other than 10%, type the 2-digit number quickly.)

Note: For Windows, the NumLock key must be on to use the keypad to set brush opacity.

Take a few moments to experiment with both of these options before you begin painting.

Selecting foreground and background colors

Adobe Photoshop uses the *foreground color* to paint, to fill selections, and as the beginning color for gradient fills. The *background color* is displayed when you delete pixels in a transparent area of color, and as the ending color for gradient fills. Think of the background color as the canvas behind a painting—when you remove paint, the canvas shows through.

The default foreground color is black, and the default background color is white. The current foreground and background colors are shown in the *color selection boxes* in the toolbox.

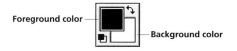

Clicking the *Switch Colors icon* reverses the colors. Clicking the *Default Colors icon* returns the foreground color to black and the background color to white.

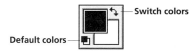

Take a few moments to try the color selection box options.

Adding detail to the line drawing

You'll begin working with the pencil tool to add detail to the cactus in the line drawing. The pencil tool draws hard-edged lines.

1 Select the pencil tool (∅) in the toolbox. You draw with the pencil tool in the same way that you draw with a pencil on paper.

2 Draw some detail lines and prickly stems to add detail to the cactus.

Note: *If you don't like your results, you can use the Undo command to undo your last stroke or you can use the eraser tool to erase multiple strokes.*

Next, you'll extend the horizon line using the line tool.

3 In the toolbox, double-click the line tool (\). For Line Width, enter a value of 2.

4 Hold down Shift, and drag to extend the horizon line from the edge of the cactus to the edge of the drawing. Holding down Shift constrains the line to a straight line.

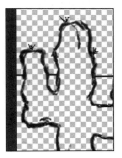

Select a new foreground color

Next, you'll select a new foreground color from the Swatches palette and paint the coyote.

The Swatches palette contains 122 color swatches from the default Adobe Photoshop palette. To select a foreground color, you click the desired swatch. When you click a color swatch, the new color appears in the foreground color selection box in the toolbox.

1 Click the Swatches palette tab to bring the palette to the front of its group. (If the palette is not visible, choose Window > Show Swatches.)

2 Click one of the brown swatches that appeals to you; the foreground swatch in the toolbox is updated to reflect the change.

3 In the toolbox, select the magic wand tool.

4 Click within the coyote's body. Then hold down Shift and click within the coyote's head and tail.

When you select an area, any painting you do affects only the area within the selection. By selecting the area within the coyote first, you won't get any paint outside the edges of the selection.

Before you begin painting, you'll create a new layer on which to paint so you can edit your painting repeatedly without affecting the black-and-white line drawing.

5 In the Layers palette, click the new layer button.

6 Double-click the layer, enter the name **Painting**, and then click OK to rename the layer.

Now you'll paint within the selection of the coyote using the paintbrush tool.

7 In the toolbox, double-click the paint-brush tool (✐) to select it and to open its Options palette.

8 Make sure that the opacity is set to 100% in the Paintbrush Options palette.

9 Paint a few areas within the coyote selection (don't fill in the selection completely).

Notice that where you applied the brown paint at an opacity level of 100%, the checkerboard is no longer visible.

10 Now drag the Opacity slider to about 60% in the Paintbrush Options palette.

11 Select another shade of brown (or any other color you like) and continue painting within the selection until you've painted the entire selection.

Notice that where you painted with the brown color at 60% opacity, part of the checkerboard shows through, indicating partial transparency.

12 Choose Select > None to deselect.

13 Choose Filter > Blur > Gaussian Blur.

Make sure that the Preview option is turned on and then experiment by dragging the Radius slider to the right. The higher the value in the Radius text box, the more blurred the colors in the selection. Click OK to apply the blur.

At this point, you'll turn off the checkerboard so you can easily see the changes you make.

14 Choose File > Preferences > Transparency & Gamut. For Grid Size, choose None; then click OK.

15 Now that you've painted the coyote, drag the Painting layer down to position it below the Drawing layer in the Layers palette (so that the outline of the coyote remains black).

Painting with the airbrush

The airbrush tool applies paint in the same way as a traditional airbrush. The default opacity for the airbrush tool is 50%, but the rate at which you drag the tool also influences the density of the paint. The more slowly you drag, the more dense the application of the paint.

You'll paint the clouds using the airbrush tool. To choose colors for the clouds, you'll select them from the Swatches palette and from the existing colors in the border of the drawing. Choosing a color within an image is called *sampling* a color. You can save sampled colors for future use by storing them in the Swatches palette.

1 In the Layers palette, make sure that the Painting layer is the active layer (so you can paint without affecting the black-and-white line drawing).

2 Click the Brushes tab and select a small soft-edged brush from the first row of brushes.

3 Double-click the airbrush tool (✎) in the toolbox to select the tool and its Options palette. Notice that the default pressure for the airbrush tool is 50%.

4 In the Swatches palette, click a gray swatch and paint a portion of the clouds using the airbrush. Don't worry if you paint a bit outside the outlines of the clouds.

Next, you'll sample a color from the border of the image to add as a color for the clouds.

5 With the airbrush tool still selected, hold down Option (Macintosh) or Alt (Windows). The pointer becomes the eyedropper (✐).

6 Click the eyedropper in the green border to sample the green color and to make it the new foreground color.

7 Release Option/Alt. The pointer becomes the airbrush tool again. Continue painting the clouds with the airbrush tool.

Note: Although you can always select the eyedropper tool from the toolbox to sample a color, you can select the eyedropper tool using Option (Macintosh) or Alt (Windows) whenever a painting tool is selected.

Before you select another color, you'll save the green color in the Swatches palette.

8 Click the Swatches palette tab.

9 Position the pointer in the blank area at the bottom of the Swatches palette; the pointer becomes a paint bucket.

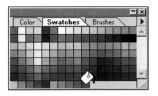

10 Click the paint bucket in the blank area; the green color is added to the Swatches palette.

Note: You don't have to save a sampled color to work with it—you've done it here just to learn how to save colors in the Swatches palette.

11 Finish painting the clouds using either sampled colors or colors from the Swatches palette.

As a final touch, you'll use the smudge tool to smudge the colors in the clouds. The smudge tool moves and mixes different colored pixels as you drag.

12 Select the smudge tool (🖑) and drag to create swirls in the clouds.

Creating gradients

As you learned in Lesson 5, "Layer Basics," a gradient is a gradual transition from one color to another over the length of a selection. You can choose from several predefined gradients in the Gradient Options palette, or you can create your own gradients.

You'll create your own gradient and apply it to the cactus.

1 In the Layers palette, make sure that the Painting layer is the active layer.

2 In the toolbox, double-click the lasso tool (🅾) to select the tool and its Options palette.

3 In the Lasso Options palette, enter a value of 3 in the Feather text box.

4 Create a rough selection around the cactus using the cactus outline as a guide. (Don't worry if the selection is a little inside or outside the outline of the cactus, you can add to or subtract from the selection later.)

5 End the selection by crossing the starting point.

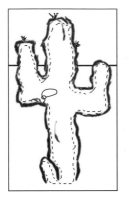

6 Double-click the gradient tool (▦) in the toolbox.

7 In the Gradient Tool Options palette, for Gradient select a gradient that appeals to you. A sample of the gradient you select appears at the bottom of the Gradient palette.

8 Drag the gradient tool from the bottom of the cactus to the top of the cactus. The gradient is applied within the selection.

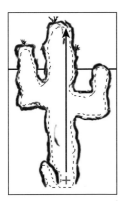

9 Choose Select > None to deselect.

Next, you'll apply a radial gradient to the sun.

10 Select the ellipse marquee tool (◌) in the toolbox. If it is not visible, choose it from the hidden tools under the rectangle marquee tool (▢).

11 In the Marquee Options palette, enter a value of 2 in the Feather text box.

12 Hold down Option (Macintosh) or Alt (Windows) key and then drag from the center point of the sun to the outside edge to create a circular selection.

13 Click the gradient tool in the toolbox. In the Gradient Tool Options palette, for Gradient choose Orange, Yellow, Orange; for Type choose Radial.

14 Drag from the center of the sun to the outside edge to apply the gradient.

15 Choose Select > None to deselect everything.

Making paint fade

You can use the Fade option to cause paint to fade to the background color or to fade to transparent over the length of a brush stroke. You'll use this option to create rays around the sun.

First, you'll learn another way to select a foreground color using the Color palette. The Color palette contains sliders and a color bar that let you change the foreground and background colors. The current foreground and background colors are displayed in the Color palette; the swatch with the outline determines which swatch is selected.

1 Click the Color palette tab to bring it to the front of the palette group.

2 Make sure that the swatch in the top left corner of the Color palette is selected. When a swatch is selected, it has a border.

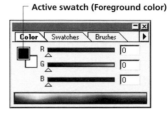

Note: If the swatch is already selected and you click it, you'll open the Adobe Photoshop Color Picker. If necessary, click Cancel to close the Color Picker.

You can select colors in the Color palette either by dragging the sliders or by dragging in the color bar at the bottom of the palette. You'll select a color from the color bar.

3 Position the pointer in the color bar; the pointer becomes an eyedropper.

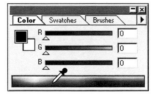

4 Just for fun, drag the eyedropper through the color bar to see how the foreground swatch changes color as you drag.

5 Select a reddish-brown color from the color bar to paint the rays around the sun.

6 Double-click the airbrush tool in the toolbox to select the tool and its Options palette.

7 In the Airbrush Options palette, turn on the Fade option and then enter a value of 15 in the Fade text box.

The value you enter in the Fade text box determines how long the painting tool will apply paint before it begins to fade. The higher the value you set, the longer the brush paints before beginning to fade.

8 Make sure that Transparent is selected in the Airbrush Options palette.

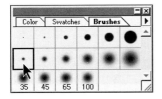

9 Click the Brushes palette tab to bring it to the front; then select a small, soft-edged brush to paint with.

10 Position the pointer in the window and drag to draw rays around the sun. You'll notice that they begin to fade as you drag.

Painting with a watercolor effect

The Wet Edges option creates a watercolor effect by building up (darkening) the edges of brush strokes. You'll paint the mountains using the Wet Edges options with the paint-brush tool.

To choose colors for the mountains, you'll use the Adobe Photoshop Color Picker. The Color Picker lets you select the foreground or background color from a color spectrum or enter values to define a color. It is also used to choose custom color systems, such as Pantone® or Focoltone® colors.

To open the Color Picker, you click the foreground or background swatch in the toolbox.

1 In the toolbox, click the foreground color swatch to open the Adobe Photoshop Color Picker.

The swatch in the top right of the Color Picker dialog box indicates the current foreground color.

New foreground color swatch
Current foreground color swatch

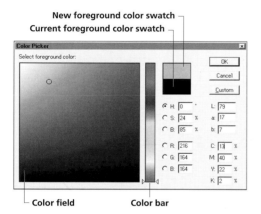

Color field   Color bar

2 Drag the triangles along the color bar to find a color range that appeals to you for painting the mountains.

As you drag, the swatch at the right side of the dialog box is updated. The top half of the swatch displays the new color, and the bottom half of the swatch displays the previous foreground or background color.

3 To select a different shade of the new color, click the desired shade in the color field at the left side of the Color Picker.

If you see an exclamation point next to a color, it means the color you have chosen is not within the range of printable colors. You'll learn more about this later.

4 To bring the color into the gamut of printable colors, click the triangle. The circle moves to the location of the closest color within the range of printable colors.

5 Click OK to close the Color Picker.

The foreground color selection box in the toolbox displays the new foreground color.

6 Double-click the paintbrush tool in the toolbox.

7 In the Paintbrush Options palette, turn on the Wet Edges option.

8 Move the paintbrush into the window and begin painting the mountains. Don't worry if you paint a little outside the edges of the mountains. You'll have a chance to clean up any stray paint in the next section.

If you'd like to paint with some straight lines, hold down Shift as you drag the paintbrush.

9 Select a variety of foreground colors to add different colors to the mountains as you paint.

10 Choose File > Save to save your work.

Making changes

You use the eraser tool to delete pixels in a drawing. Depending on the option you choose, you can erase all of the pixels in an area, or you erase only the pixels that were not saved with the last version of the image.

1 Click the eraser tool (⌀) in the toolbox and move the pointer into the image area. By default, the eraser is the same shape and size as the default paintbrush.

2 Drag the eraser tool over any area around the mountains where you want to erase any stray paint.

Applying a background to the drawing

To add a background to the drawing, you'll create a new layer and apply two gradients—one for the sky and one for the ground.

1 In the Layers palette, click the New Layer button to add a new layer.

2 Double-click the layer, enter the name **Gradients**, and click OK.

3 Drag the Gradients layer to the bottom of the Layers palette, to position it behind the rest of the artwork.

4 Select the rectangle marquee tool (⬚) in the toolbox. Drag a selection marquee from the horizon line to the top of the image.

5 Select a foreground color and a background color that appeal to you. In the Gradient palette, for Type, make sure that Foreground to Background is selected.

6 Select the gradient tool (▨) in the toolbox.

7 Drag from the top of the image to the horizon line to apply it to the selection.

Note: The length of the line you draw with the gradient tool determines how gradient colors are applied. If you draw a short line with the gradient tool, a sharp transition from one color to the next occurs. The longer the line you draw, the softer the transition from one color to another.

8 Choose Select > Inverse to select the opposite area of the image (the ground).

9 To apply a gradient to the ground, either select a new foreground color and background color, or select a predefined gradient from the Gradient Options palette.

10 Drag from the bottom of the selection to the top of the selection to apply the gradient.

11 In the Layers palette, drag the Opacity slider to lower the opacity of the gradient.

Working with brushes

In addition to the round brushes, Adobe Photoshop provides several additional brush shapes you can paint with, and even lets you create your own custom brush shapes.

You'll start by painting with a star-shaped brush, and then you'll create your own brush shape to add a final lizardy touch to your drawing!

1 In the Layers palette, make sure that the Painting layer is the active layer.

2 Click the Brushes palette tab; then choose Load Brushes from the Brushes menu.

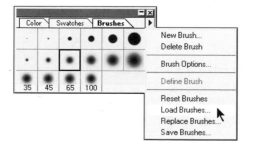

3 In the Lesson06 folder, select Assorted.abr and then click Open to add the custom brushes to the Brushes palette.

Note: For this lesson, we've placed the custom brushes in the Lesson06 folder. For future reference, the custom brushes are located in the Goodies/Brushes/Assorted Brushes folder (Macintosh) or Photoshop subdirectory (Windows).

4 In the toolbox, click the Switch Colors icon in the color selection box area to swap the default colors: white becomes the foreground color.

Switch Colors icon

5 Select one of the star brushes and add some stars to the sky. If desired, vary the opacity of the stars by changing the opacity level in the Paintbrush Options palette.

Next, you'll define your own brush and use it to create a footprint in the desert.

6 Choose File > Open. In the Lesson06 folder, select Gecko.psd and click Open.

You can create a brush shape from any selection.

7 Choose Select > All to select the entire image; then choose Define Brush from the Brushes menu. The gecko footprint is added to the Brushes palette.

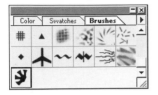

8 Double-click the gecko brush. In the Brush Options dialog box, enter **200** in the Spacing text box; then click OK.

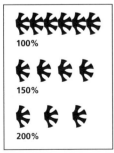

The amount you enter for brush spacing controls the distance between brush strokes.

100%

150%

200%

Brush spacing set to different values

9 Select a green color from the border of the drawing by holding down Option (Macintosh) or Alt (Windows), and sampling the color from the border.

10 In the Paintbrush Options palette, enter a Fade rate of 8.

11 Drag to create a footprint in the desert that fades over length of the brush stroke.

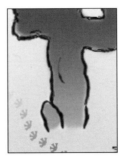

12 Choose File > Save to save your artwork. You've completed the painting lesson. You're well on your way to learning Adobe Photoshop!

Review

• What is the benefit of making a selection before starting to paint in an area?

• Why is it important to understand the relationship between a painting tool, its Options palette, and the Brushes palette?

• How can you display a painting tool by its size in pixels?

• How do you create a custom brush?

A

Project A

Creating a CD Cover

Once you've learned the basic techniques for selecting, painting, and layering, you can begin to focus on using Adobe Photoshop as a design tool. You'll use the techniques you've learned, plus a few new ones, to design and create a CD cover.

In this lesson, you'll learn how to do the following:

• Use the Info palette to measure a selection.

• Set the marquee tool to a constrained size to make selections of the same shape.

• Select blending modes to apply various color effects to parts of an image.

• Use the type tool and the type mask tool to create type.

• Paint type while preserving the transparent areas around the type.

• Use the Brightness/Contrast command to adjust a selection.

Restoring default preferences

Before starting this lesson, delete the Adobe Photoshop Preferences file to restore the program's default palettes and command settings. If you need step-by-step instructions about how to delete the preferences file, see "Restoring default preferences" on page 4.

Restart Adobe Photoshop.

Getting started

Before you begin working, you'll open the finished art file and look at the completed image to get an idea of what you'll create.

1 Choose File > Open. Locate and open the ProjectA folder, then select EndA.psd and click Open.

An image of a CD cover appears.

2 If desired, choose View > Zoom Out to make the image smaller and leave it on your screen as you work. If you don't want to leave the image open, choose File > Close.

Now you'll open a partially completed file, to which you'll add images and type to complete the CD cover.

3 Choose File > Open. Locate and open the ProjectA folder, then select StartA.psd and click Open.

4 Choose File > Save As, enter the name WorkA.psd, and click Save.

Using the Info palette

The Info palette displays information about the location of the pointer in the image window, as well as information about the size of selections and the color values in an image. Depending on the tool you're using and the action you're performing, the Info palette may display additional information, such as the selection's angle of rotation.

You'll use the Info palette to measure a selection, and then use the information to set an aspect ratio option for the marquee tool.

1 Click the Info palette tab to bring the palette to the front of the group. (If the palette is hidden, choose Window > Show Info.)

2 Choose Palette Options from the Info palette menu.

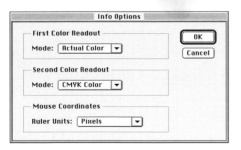

3 In the Mouse Coordinates section of the Info Options dialog box, select pixels as the unit of measurement.

Note: You can use any unit of measure you're comfortable with; in this example, we've used pixels.

4 Click OK to close the dialog box.

5 Select the zoom tool (🔍) in the toolbox, then click the zoom tool once on the flower in the upper right corner to magnify its view.

6 Select the marquee tool (▢) in the toolbox, and move the pointer into the window. The pointer becomes a crosshair.

Sometimes it can be difficult to get an accurate measurement using the default tool pointer. To display a tool's *hot spot*—the point from which any action takes place—you can turn on the Precise Cursor option by pressing the Caps Lock key.

7 Press the Caps Lock key to turn on precise cursors. You'll notice a single pixel at the center of the marquee crosshairs (⊹), indicating the tool's hot spot.

8 Position the pointer hot spot at the top left corner of the flower, and drag diagonally to the lower right corner to select the flower.

To adjust the position of the selection marquee over the flower while creating the selection marquee, hold down the Spacebar and drag as you draw the marquee and before releasing the mouse.

9 As you drag, watch the W(idth) and H(eight) values in the Info palette. Once you've selected the flower, the width and height should be the same (a square).

When a selection is square, it has a 1:1 aspect ratio, meaning that the width and height are identical. You'll set a 1:1 aspect ratio in the Marquee Options palette to select the remaining flowers for the CD cover.

10 Choose Select > None to deselect the artwork.

11 Double-click the zoom tool in the tool-box to return the display of the image to actual size.

12 Select the marquee tool in the toolbox. In the Marquee Options palette, for Style, choose Constrained Aspect Ratio. The default ratio is 1:1.

You'll open and select two additional flowers for the CD cover using the constrained aspect ratio, ensuring that each selection is square.

13 Choose File > Open, locate and select Dahlia.psd in the ProjectA folder; then click Open. If necessary, reposition the window so you can see part of both windows.

14 Using the rectangle marquee tool, drag diagonally from the top left corner of the flower to the lower right corner. (You won't be able to select the entire flower because the Constrained Aspect Ratio option is turned on, allowing you to select only a square area.)

15 To adjust the position of the selection marquee after drawing it, press the Shift and arrow keys to move to the right or the left in 10-pixel increments, or position the pointer within the selection and drag to reposition the marquee.

16 Note the values in the Info palette; the width and height of the selection are identical.

17 Select the move tool (✢) in the toolbox and drag the dahlia into the CD window.

18 With the move tool still selected, drag the flower into the lower right corner of the CD window to align it at the bottom right corner of the image.

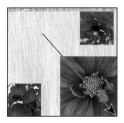

Once you've positioned the flower approximately where you want it, use the arrow keys to align it precisely.

At the top of the Layers palette, a new layer named Layer 1 appears. Each time you move a selection from one image to another using the drag-and-drop method, a new layer is created automatically for the selection.

19 In the Layers palette, double-click Layer 1, rename it Dahlia, and then click OK.

20 Close the Dahlia.psd file and do not save changes.

21 Choose File > Save to save your work.

Changing the size of an image

The Image Size command lets you change the dimensions and resolution of an image. For this part of the project, you'll open a flower image and resize it to fit the CD cover. The CD cover and image have the same image resolution, so you won't need to adjust that. For information about changing the resolution of an image, see "What is resolution, and how does it affect an image?" on page 27.

Choose File > Open. Locate and select Rose.psd in the ProjectA folder; then click Open. If necessary, reposition the window so you can see part of both windows.

1 Choose Image > Image Size.

In the Pixel Dimensions section of the dialog box, the link icon to the right of the Width and Height text boxes indicates that the width and height of the image are proportionately linked. If the value in either of the text boxes is changed, both values change. The Constrain Proportions option at the bottom of the dialog box controls the link between the width, height, and resolution of an image.

Constrain proportions   Link icon

2 For Height, enter **188**. The value in the Height field is automatically adjusted, as are the values in the Print Size section of the dialog box.

3 Click OK to resize the rose image.

4 Select the move tool in the toolbox, position the pointer in the Rose.psd window, and then drag the rose into the CD cover window.

5 Align the rose with the top left corner of the flower located in the upper right corner of the image.

6 If necessary, select the zoom tool in the toolbox, and drag a marquee around the top right corner of the rose to zoom in and verify that the rose is properly aligned.

7 If you need to adjust the rose, hold down Command (Macintosh) or Ctrl (Windows) and press the arrow keys.

💡 When a tool other than the move tool is selected and you want to use the arrow keys to move a selection, hold down Command (Macintosh) or Ctrl (Windows) to select the move tool from the keyboard; then press the arrow keys to move the selection.

Again, a new layer named Layer 1 appears at the top of the Layers palette.

8 In the Layers palette, double-click the new layer, rename it Rose, and click OK.

9 Close the Rose.psd file, and do not save changes.

10 In the Layers palette, drag the Rose layer below the Dahlia layer to reposition the rose behind the dahlia.

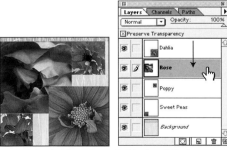

Repositioning Rose layer behind Dahlia layer

11 Choose File > Save to save your work.

Using blending modes

At this point, you've combined all the elements of the CD cover into a single image. Now you'll paint the flowers using a variety of painting tools and blending modes. For a color sample of all the blending modes, see A–1 in the color section of this book.

In Lesson 5, "Layer Basics," you learned about selecting modes for layers to produce different effects on individual layers. You can also select modes for painting tools, called *blending modes,* for different effects. When selecting blending modes, it's helpful to think of the effects in terms of the following three colors:

• The *base color* is the color of the pixels in the original image.

• The *blend color* is the color you're painting with (the current foreground color).

• The *result color* is the color produced when the base and blend colors are mixed.

1 In the Layers palette, make the Poppy layer the active layer.

Next, you'll select the artwork on the Poppy layer using a shortcut.

2 In the Layers palette, Command+click (Macintosh) or Ctrl+click (Windows) the Poppy layer.

When you use this keyboard sequence to create a selection, only the areas containing pixel values (in this case, the poppy image) are selected. Any areas that don't have pixel values are considered transparent and are not selected.

3 Click the Swatches tab to display the Swatches palette; then click a color that appeals to you.

4 Choose Edit > Fill, for Mode select Color, enter 70 in the Opacity text box, and then click OK.

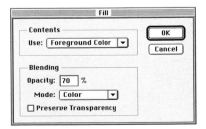

The Color blending mode adds the luminance of the original color in the image to the hue and saturation of the blend color (the color you selected from the Swatches palette). The Color mode preserves the gray levels in the image and is useful for coloring grayscale images.

5 Choose Select > None to deselect everything.

6 Choose File > Save to save your work.

7 In the Layers palette, make the Dahlia layer the active layer.

8 Double-click the lasso tool ($\wp$) in the toolbox. In the Marquee Options palette, set a Feather value of 1.

9 Using the lasso tool, drag a fairly accurate selection around the center of the flower.

10 In the Swatches palette, select a yellow foreground color. You'll use this color to paint the flower's center.

11 Choose File > Preferences > Display & Cursors. For Painting Cursors, select Brush Size, and then click OK.

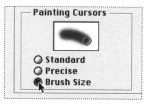

12 Double-click the paintbrush tool (ℓ) in the toolbox. In the Paintbrush Options palette, set the opacity to about 50%, for Mode select Color.

13 Paint the center of the flower using the paintbrush.

Again, the Color mode maintains the luminance of the pixels in the underlying image while replacing the hue and saturation with the yellow color you selected.

14 Choose File > Save to save your work.

Saving a selection

You can save selections for later use. You'll save the flower selection.

1 Choose Select > Save Selection. For Channel, choose New.

```
┌─────────── Save Selection ───────────┐
│ ┌─ Destination ─────────────┐         │
│ │ Document: [Work06a.psd ▼] │ ┌─ OK ─┐│
│ │                           │ └──────┘│
│ │ Channel: [ New      ] [▼] │┌Cancel┐ │
│ │                           │└──────┘ │
│ └───────────────────────────┘         │
│ ┌─ Operation ─────────────┐           │
│ │ ● New Channel           │           │
│ │ ○ Add to Channel        │           │
│ │ ○ Subtract from Channel │           │
│ │ ○ Intersect with Channel│           │
│ └─────────────────────────┘           │
└───────────────────────────────────────┘
```

2 Click OK to save the selection. You'll use this selection in a moment.

When you save a selection, it is automatically given a numeric name and stored in a channel. In this case, you're working in an RGB image and the numbers 1, 2, and 3 are taken by the red, green, and blue channels, so number 4 is the next available number.

3 In the Layers palette, Command+click (Macintosh) or Ctrl+click (Windows) the Dahlia layer to load the dahlia as a selection.

Now you'll subtract the center selection you saved from the current selection to make the petals of the flower the active selection.

4 Choose Select > Load Selection, and then choose #4 from the Channel menu.

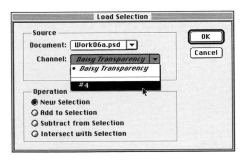

5 In the Operation section of the Load Selection dialog box, choose Subtract from Selection. This option will subtract the selection you saved (#4) from the active selection, resulting in a selection containing only the flower petals.

```
┌─────────── Load Selection ───────────┐
│ ┌─ Source ──────────────────┐         │
│ │ Document: [Work06a.psd ▼] │ ┌─ OK ─┐│
│ │                           │ └──────┘│
│ │ Channel: [ #4        ] [▼]│┌Cancel┐ │
│ │           □ Invert        │└──────┘ │
│ └───────────────────────────┘         │
│ ┌─ Operation ──────────────┐          │
│ │ ○ New Selection          │          │
│ │ ○ Add to Selection       │          │
│ │ ● Subtract from Selection│          │
│ │ ○ Intersect with Selection│         │
│ └──────────────────────────┘          │
└───────────────────────────────────────┘
```

6 Click OK. The center of the selection has been subtracted, leaving only the outer portion of the dahlia selected.

You'll learn more about channels in Lesson 7, "Masks and Channels."

Now, you'll paint the flower petals.

7 Select a new foreground color from the Swatches palette for the flower petals.

8 In the Paintbrush Options palette, set the opacity to about 50% and choose the Multiply mode.

The Multiply mode multiplies the base color by the blend color. Each time you paint over a part of the image, the color is built up, resulting in a darker color.

9 Click the Brushes palette tab and select a large, soft-edged brush. (If necessary, turn off the Caps Lock key.)

10 With the paintbrush tool, paint the petals without lifting the brush.

11 Now choose a smaller soft-edged brush from the Brushes palette, and paint around the inside edges of the petals to multiply (darken) the paint color.

12 Choose Select > None to deselect everything.

13 Choose File > Save to save your work.

Creating a gradient

Now, you'll create your own gradient and apply it to the rose image.

1 Using colors from the Swatches palette, select a foreground color and background color that appeal to you. (To select a background color, hold down Option (Macintosh) or Alt (Windows) before clicking a color in the Swatches palette.)

2 Double-click the gradient tool (▓) in the toolbox.

3 In the Gradient Options palette, for Gradient, choose Foreground to Background. Set the Opacity to 55%, for mode, choose Color, and for Type, choose Radial.

4 In the Layers palette, select the Rose layer; then Command+click (Macintosh) or Ctrl+click (Windows) to load the rose as the selection.

5 Drag the gradient tool from the center of the rose to the outside edge of the selection.

The gradient you created is applied to the rose selection.

6 Choose Select > None to deselect everything; then choose File > Save to save your work.

Now you'll continue painting the other flowers.

7 In the Layers palette, select the Sweet Peas layer; then Command+click (Macintosh) or Ctrl+click (Windows) the layer to load the sweet peas as a selection.

8 Choose a new foreground color that appeals to you.

9 Double-click the paintbrush tool in the toolbox.

10 In the Paintbrush Options palette, for mode, choose Screen.

The Screen mode multiplies the opposite of the original image color with the selected painting color, to produce a lighter color.

11 Set the Opacity to about 60%.

12 In the Brushes palette, choose a large soft-edged brush and then paint the Sweet Peas.

13 Choose Select > None to deselect everything.

Merging layers

To complete the flower compositions, you'll merge the individual flower layers onto a single layer and then outline them. Merging layers reduces the size of a file, but shouldn't be done until you've finalized design decisions and finished editing individual layers within the image.

There are two ways to merge layers. You can either merge all the visible layers, or you can use the Merge Down command to merge one layer at a time. You'll use both of these methods to get an idea of how merging works.

1 In the Layers palette, select the Dahlia layer to make it the active layer.

2 Choose Merge Down from the Layers palette menu. The Dahlia layer is merged with the Rose layer.

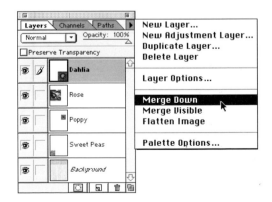

To use the Merge Visible command, you turn off the layers you don't want included in the merge operation.

3 Click the eye icon next to the Background to turn it off; then choose Merge Visible from the Layers palette menu.

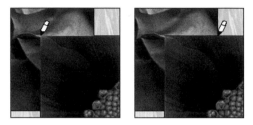

4 Click the eye icon next to the Background to make it visible.

5 Double-click the remaining flower layer (Rose), name it Flowers, and then click OK.

Now you'll add a border to all the flowers.

6 In the Layers palette, click the New Layer button to create a new layer; then double-click the layer, rename it Outlines, and click OK.

7 In the Layers palette, Command+click (Macintosh) or Ctrl+click (Windows) the Flowers layer to load all the flowers as a selection.

8 Click the Default Colors icon to set the foreground color and background color to their default colors (black and white).

9 Choose Edit > Stroke. For Width, choose 1 pixel; for Location, choose Center. Click OK to draw a border around the flowers.

10 Choose Select > None to deselect everything.

To add the border where the images intersect, you'll use the pencil tool.

11 Click the zoom tool in the toolbox, and then click once over the area where the two large flowers intersect.

12 From the toolbox, select the pencil tool ($\mathscr{l}$). Click the pencil at the top left corner of the dahlia where the flowers intersect; then hold down Shift, and click to the right where the first border ends.

13 Repeat the previous step to add the border along the left side of the image.

14 Choose File > Save to save your work.

Adding canvas around an image

Now you'll add some area around the flowers to make room for the name of the CD. Using the Canvas Size command, you can increase the area around an image without changing the size or resolution of the image data.

1 Choose Image > Canvas Size. Select Pixels from the menu to the right of the Width text box; then for Width, enter 350. Click the middle square in the far right row to indicate that the image should be positioned to the right of the added area; then click OK.

You'll create a new layer for the border and fill it with black, and then add type to the border.

2 In the Layers palette, click the New Layer button, name the layer Border, and then click OK.

3 Double-click the rectangle marquee tool in the toolbox. In the Marquee Options palette, choose Normal for Style.

4 Drag a marquee the size of the new area to select it.

5 Select the paint bucket tool (✋) in the toolbox. Then click within the rectangular selection to fill it with black (the current foreground color).

6 Choose Select > None to deselect everything; then choose File > Save to save your work.

Adding type

To complete the CD cover, you'll add type to the cover and paint the type. When you create type in Adobe Photoshop, it is automatically placed on a separate layer.

1 In the Layers palette, make sure that the top layer (the Border layer) is selected.

2 Click the Switch Colors icon in the toolbox to make the foreground color white and the background color black.

3 Click the type tool in the toolbox; then position it near the top left area of the black border and click. The Type dialog box appears.

4 Select a font and size (We used 6-point Eccentric.) Type **The** in the text box at the bottom of the dialog box, and then click OK. The type is placed on its own layer and is added to the image.

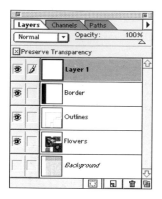

5 Press Command (Macintosh) or Ctrl (Windows) to select the move tool, drag the type into position at the top left area of the black border.

To select the move tool without deselecting the type tool, hold down Command (Macintosh) or Ctrl (Windows), and drag.

6 Position the type tool under the word *The* and click to open the Type dialog box.

7 Select the Vertical Centered text option. Choose a font and size for the type. (We used 14-point Eccentric.) Type **Archive** and click OK.

8 Drag the type or press the arrow keys on the keyboard to nudge the type into place.

9 Each time you add type, a new layer is created in the Layers palette. To merge the two type layers, choose Merge Down from the Layers menu. Both words are now on the same layer.

As a final step, you'll paint type with different colors from the artwork.

10 In the Layers palette, make sure that the Preserve Transparency option is selected for the Type layer.

The Preserve Transparency option lets you paint only where there are already pixel values on the layer. In this case, with the Preserve Transparency option selected, you'll only be able to paint on the type.

11 Select the eyedropper tool (✐) in the toolbox; then click a color you like in the artwork. The color becomes the foreground color.

12 Double-click the paintbrush tool in the toolbox. In the Paintbrush Options palette, set the Opacity to 100% and for mode, choose Normal.

13 Use the paintbrush tool to paint individual letters of the *Archive* text.

14 To create multicolored text, paint a small amount with one color and then sample another color using the eyedropper tool and continue painting.

You can switch between a painting tool and the eyedropper tool as you paint by pressing the Option (Macintosh) or Alt (Windows) key.

15 Choose File > Save to save your work.

As a final step, you'll use the type mask tool, which lets you create type that has a selection outline, but no fill color. When you use the type mask tool, only the selection appears on-screen. (it is not filled with the foreground color).

You'll position the type mask on the background, and then adjust the brightness and contrast of the background to make it appear through the type mask for a textured effect.

16 In the Layers palette, select the Background.

17 Select the type mask tool (☂) from the hidden tools palette under the type tool.

18 Click the type mask tool about 2 inches to the left of the top right corner.

19 In the Type dialog box, select a horizontal type option; enter a font size of about 8, and then type **Volume I** in the text box. Click OK.

The type mask appears on the Background. If you need to reposition the type, position the pointer anywhere within the type outline and drag.

Note: When you use the type mask tool, the type mask is added to the selected layer in the Layers palette.

20 Choose Image > Adjust > Brightness/Contrast. Enter −27 in the Brightness text box and **50** in the Contrast text box. The brightness and contrast of the reeds are adjusted and show through the type outline.

21 Click OK.

22 To preview the adjustment without deselecting, choose View > Hide Edges.

23 If you're satisfied with the results, choose View > Show Edges to see the selection and then choose Select > None to deselect everything.

24 In the Layers palette, choose Flatten Image to flatten the file into a single layer and to reduce the file size.

25 Choose File > Save to save your work.

You've completed the CD cover image. If desired, open the WorkA.psd file and rebuild the CD cover, but this time select other blending modes to see what other effects you create when you paint the flowers.

7

Lesson 7
Masks and Channels

Adobe Photoshop uses masks to isolate and manipulate specific parts of an image. A mask is like a stencil: The cutout portion of the mask can be altered, but the area surrounding the cutout is protected from change. You can create a temporary mask for one-time use, or you can save masks for repeated use. As a general rule, it's a good idea to save a mask if you plan to work on a specific area of an image more than once.

In this lesson, you'll learn how to do the following:

- Refine a partial selection using a quick mask.

- Save a selection as a mask.

- Load a saved mask.

- View a mask in a channel.

- Paint in a mask to modify a selection.

Restoring default preferences

Before starting this lesson, delete the Adobe Photoshop Preferences file to restore the program's default palettes and command settings. For step-by-step instructions about how to delete the preferences file, see "Restoring default preferences" on page 4.

Restart Adobe Photoshop.

Getting started

Before you begin working, you'll open the finished art to get an idea of what you'll create.

1 Choose File > Open. Locate and open the Lesson07 folder, then select End07.psd and click Open.

An image of an egret appears.

2 If desired, choose View > Zoom Out to make the image smaller and leave it on your screen as you work. If you don't want to leave the image open on your screen, choose File > Close.

You'll begin by opening a photograph of an egret, and then work with masks and channels to edit the image.

1 Choose File > Open. Locate and open the Lesson07 folder, then select Start07.psd and click Open.

2 Choose File > Save As, enter the name Work07.psd, and click Save.

Using quick masks

The Adobe Photoshop Quick Mask option lets you create temporary masks, which are discarded once the mask has been converted to a selection.

When you apply a quick mask to a partial selection, everything that is not selected is masked (hidden), and everything that is selected is visible. The parts of the image that are masked are covered with a red-colored overlay, which is like a traditional rubylith overlay. (You can make the overlay any color, but for now you'll work with red, the default color.) To see an image of the egret with a selection marquee and the egret isolated using a quick mask, see illustration 7–1 in the color section of this book.

To add to or subtract from a selection in Quick Mask mode, you "paint" or "erase" the red overlay color using the default foreground and background colors, black and white.

Painting with white *erases* the red overlay color, thereby *increasing* the selected area.

Painting with black *adds* red to the overlay, thereby *decreasing* the selected area.

Applying a quick mask

You'll begin by making a partial selection of the egret using the magic wand tool, and then you'll edit the selection using a quick mask.

Note: *A partial selection must exist to see the overlay color in Quick Mask mode.*

1 Double-click the magic wand tool (✎) in the toolbox to select the tool and its Options palette.

2 In the Magic Wand Options palette, for Tolerance, enter a value of 16.

3 Click anywhere in the white area of the egret to begin the selection process.

4 Hold down Shift and click the magic wand on another white portion of the egret to extend the selection. You'll notice that when you hold down Shift, a plus sign appears next to the magic wand tool, indicating that it is adding to the selection.

At this point, some of the egret isn't selected. Don't add anymore to the selection because you'll add to it using a quick mask.

5 In the toolbox, click the Quick Mask icon.

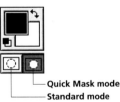

A red overlay appears over the parts of the image that were not selected with the magic wand tool. This overlay color depicts the hidden, or masked areas, in the image.

Now you'll refine the selection of the egret by "painting" on the mask.

Painting a quick mask

Adobe Photoshop uses black and white to identify the hidden and visible areas in a mask. In Quick Mask mode, the red overlay color is equal to black and the transparent areas are equal to white. Where the mask is red (black), the underlying artwork is not selected; where the mask is transparent (white), the artwork is visible, or selected. To see how painting with black and white affects a quick mask, see the series of illustrations in section 7–2 of the color portion of this book.

You'll begin by painting with white to increase the selected area within the egret. As you work with the egret image, you'll move back and forth between Quick Mask mode and Standard mode to see exactly how painting in the mask alters the selected area.

1 Click the Switch Colors icon above the foreground and background swatches in the toolbox to make white the foreground color.

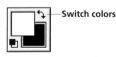
Switch colors

2 Choose Preferences > Display and Cursors. In the Painting Cursors section of the dialog box, select the Brush Size option and click OK.

3 Click the paintbrush tool (✐) in the toolbox; then click the Brushes palette tab and select a medium brush from the first row of brushes.

4 Move the paintbrush onto the window and begin painting over the red areas within the egret's body. As you paint with white, the red areas are erased.

5 If desired, zoom in on the image by selecting the zoom tool from the keyboard. Hold down Command+Spacebar (Macintosh) or Ctrl+Spacebar (Windows) to select the zoom-in tool; then release the keys to go back to painting.

As you erase the red parts of the mask by painting with white, don't worry if you paint outside the outline of the egret's body. You'll have a chance to make corrections in a minute.

6 Click the Standard Mode icon to move from Quick Mask mode back to the selection.

Standard mode

Notice that the selection marquee has increased, selecting more of the egret's body.

7 Double-click the zoom tool in the toolbox to return to a 100% view of the egret.

8 Click the Quick Mask icon again to return to the masked view, and continue painting with white to erase the remainder of the mask (red) in the egret, including its beak and legs. If necessary, use the zoom tool to zoom in on parts of the bird.

9 Click the Standard Mode icon to move from Quick Mask mode back to the selection.

Note that using a quick mask to create a selection is similar to creating a selection using a combination of the magic wand tool and the lasso tool.

If there are areas within the body of the egret that appear to still be selected, it means that you haven't erased all of the mask.

10 If necessary, go back to Quick Mask mode and erase the remaining parts of the mask.

Selection in Standard mode   *Erasing in Quick Mask mode*

11 Once you've erased all of the red areas within the egret, click the Standard Mode icon again. The entire egret is selected!

12 Choose File > Save to save your work.

At this point, if you've erased the mask outside the edges of the egret, and subsequently included part of the background in the selection, you'll return to Quick Mask mode and restore the mask to those edge areas by painting with the mask color (red).

13 Click the Quick Mask icon to return to Quick Mask mode.

14 Click the Switch Colors icon at the corner of the foreground and background swatches in the toolbox to make black (which will paint as red in Quick Mask mode) the foreground color.

15 From the Brushes palette, select a small brush from the first row of brushes.

You'll paint the mask back in where you erased too much of it around the edges of the egret.

16 Using the zoom tool, zoom in on an area where you need to repaint the mask.

17 Select the paintbrush tool and repaint the mask where you need to.

18 Once you've painted the mask back in around the edges outside the egret's body, click the Standard Mode icon. Notice that the selection has been refined to better select the outline of the egret.

Although quick masks are useful for one-time tasks, they disappear once you deselect. If you've spent more than about 30 seconds

making a selection, or if you plan to work on an area repeatedly, it's a good idea to save the selection as a mask.

The next section shows you how to save a selection as a mask and then load it to make adjustments to the selection.

Saving a selection as a mask

Any selection can be saved as a mask in a channel, whether you've created it using the selection tools or using a quick mask. You'll save the selection of the egret, edit it in the channel, and then load the selection.

Masks are saved in channels, which can be thought of as storage areas in a document. When you save a selection as a mask, a new channel is created to store the mask.

1 Double-click the hand tool in the toolbox to make the egret image fit in the window.

2 Click the Channels tab to bring it to the front of its palette group. You'll see the new channel added to the Channels palette when you save your selection.

3 Choose Select > Save Selection.

For Destination, the document name appears, and by default, for Channel, the name New appears.

Editing a mask in a channel

As you learned earlier, Adobe Photoshop uses black and white to indicate which part of an image is hidden (black) and which part is selected (white).

Very often, tiny areas of an image are not included in the initial selection but can't be discerned until you look at the saved selection in a channel. You can paint directly in the channel to correct these areas.

You'll paint in the Egret channel to perfect the selection of the egret.

4 Click OK to accept the defaults. You'll rename this new channel in a moment.

The Channels palette displays a composite channel for the RGB image, and a separate channel for the red, green, and blue channels. When you saved your selection, a new channels, named #4, was added to the bottom of the Channels palette.

1 Make sure that white is the selected foreground color; then choose a small brush from the Brushes palette, and paint out any black or gray flecks within the body of the egret.

Selection in channel *Painting out black or gray*

5 Choose Select > None to deselect everything.

6 To rename the channel, double-click channel #4 in the Channels palette. Type the name **Egret** in the Channel Options dialog box, and then click OK.

2 If there are any white specks in the black area of the channel, make black the foreground color and paint those out as well.

3 Choose File > Save to save your work.

Making adjustments to a selection

Now that you've corrected any flaws in the selection by painting in the channel, you'll adjust the tonal balance of the egret and then invert the selection to add a filter to the background.

1 In the Channels palette, click the RGB composite channel to display the entire image.

Now you'll load the Egret channel as a selection.

2 Choose Select > Load Selection. For Channel, choose Egret and click OK.

The egret selection appears in the image window.

3 Choose Image > Adjust > Auto Levels. The levels in the selection are automatically adjusted.

4 Choose Select > Inverse. Now the selection is inverted and the background is selected.

5 Choose Filter > Artistic > Colored Pencil. If desired, experiment with the sliders to see the changes before you apply the filter.

If you want to preview different areas of the background, you can drag in the preview window of the Color Pencil filter dialog box. This preview option is available with all filters.

6 Click Apply when you're satisfied with the Colored Pencil settings. The filter is applied to the background selection.

7 Choose Select > None to deselect everything.

8 Choose File > Save to save your work.

You've successfully saved, loaded, and inverted a selection. Now you'll add a gradient to a channel and load it as a selection.

Adding a gradient to a channel

In addition to using black to indicate what's hidden and white to indicate what's selected, you can paint with shades of gray to indicate partial transparency. For example, if you paint in a channel with a shade of gray that is halfway between black and white, the underlying image becomes partially (50%) visible.

You'll experiment by adding a gradient (which makes a transition from black to gray to white) to a channel and then filling the selection with a color to see how the transparency levels of the black, gray, and white in the gradient affect the image.

1 In the Channels palette, create a new channel by clicking the New Channel button (⬓) at the bottom of the palette.

The new channel appears at the bottom of the Channels palette.

2 Double-click the new channel to open the Channel Options dialog box, and rename the channel Gradient. Click OK.

3 Double-click the gradient tool (▦) in the toolbox to select the tool and its Options palette.

4 In the Gradient Tool Options palette, choose Black, White from the Gradient menu.

5 Hold down Shift, and drag the gradient tool from the top of the window to the bottom of the window. The gradient is applied to the channel.

Now you'll load the gradient as a selection and fill the selection with a color.

When you load a gradient as a selection and then fill the selection with a color, the opacity of the fill color varies over the length of the gradient. Where the gradient is black, no fill color is present; where the gradient is gray, the fill color is partially visible; and where the gradient is white, the fill color is completely visible.

6 In the Channels palette, click the RGB channel to display the composite image. Next, you'll load the Gradient channel as a selection.

7 *Without* deselecting the RGB channel, position the pointer over the Gradient channel. Drag the channel to the Load Selection button at the bottom of the palette to load the gradient as a selection.

8 In the toolbox, make sure that the foreground and background colors are set to their default (black and white). If necessary, click the Default Colors icon at the bottom left corner of the color selection swatches.

A selection marquee appears in the window. Although the selection marquee appears over only about half the image, it is correct. Selection marquees are displayed based on the following pixel information: If the pixel value is 0% to 50% opaque, a selection marquee does not appear, but if the pixel value is 51% to 100% opaque, a selection marquee is displayed.

9 Press Delete to fill the gradient selection with the current background color, which is white.

10 Choose Select > None to deselect everything.

As a final step, you'll add type to the egret image to complete the artwork.

11 In the toolbox, click the type tool (**T**), and then click anywhere in the document window.

12 For Size, enter 48, and then type **Snowy Egret** in the text box. Click OK to add the type to the artwork.

13 Click the move tool in the toolbox to select it; then drag to position the type where you want it.

14 Choose File > Save to save your work.

You have completed the Masks and Channels lesson. Although it takes some practice to become comfortable using channels, you've learned all the fundamental concepts and skills you need to get started using masks and channels.

Review

• What is a quick mask?

• What happens to a quick mask when you deselect?

• When you save a selection as a mask, where is the mask stored?

• How can you edit a mask in a channel once you've saved it?

• What determines the visibility of a selection marquee when you load a selection from a channel?

Lesson 1: Finished artwork

Lesson 2: Finished artwork

2-1: Vector image versus raster image

2-2: Halftone screen using black ink

Halftone screens using process ink colors

2-3: Varying bit depths

Bitmap

Grayscale

8-bit color

24-bit color

2-4: Color gamuts

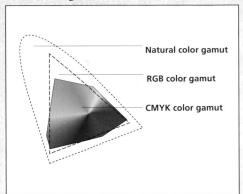

Natural color gamut

RGB color gamut

CMYK color gamut

2-5: RGB color model

Magenta

Blue

Red

White

Cyan

Yellow

Green

2-6: CMYK color model

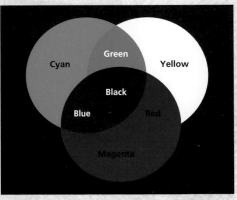

Cyan

Green

Yellow

Black

Blue

Red

Magenta

2-7: Sufficient versus insufficient resolution

225 ppi   *72 ppi*

2-8: Image resolution

*300 ppi image sampled
down to 225*

*72 ppi image sampled up
to 225 ppi*

Lesson 3: Finished artwork

Lesson 4: Finished artwork

4-1: Non-anti-aliased edge

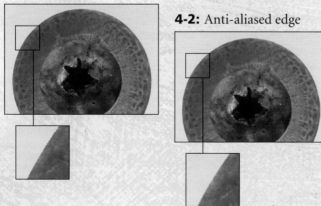

4-2: Anti-aliased edge

4-3: Feathered edge

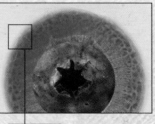

Lesson 5: Finished artwork

Lesson 6: Finished artwork

Project A: Finished artwork

5-1: Layer mode samples

Layer 1

Background

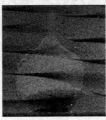

Dissolve, 50% opacity

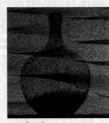

Multiply

Screen

Overlay

Soft Light

Hard Light

Color Dodge

Color Burn

Darken

Lighten

Difference

Exclusion

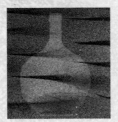

Hue

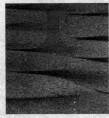

Saturation

Color

Luminosity

A-1: Application of brush stroke to background using blending modes

Normal, 100% opacity

Normal, 50% opacity

Dissolve, 50% opacity

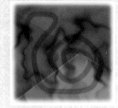

Multiply

Screen

Soft Light

Hard Light

Color Dodge

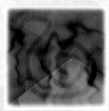

Color Burn

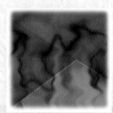

Darken

Lighten

Difference

Exclusion

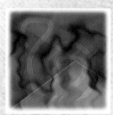

Hue

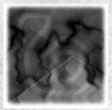

Color

Luminosity

Overlay

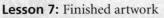

7-1: Original selection in Standard Mode and Quick Mask mode

Selected Areas

Hidden Areas

7-2: Painting in quick mask mode

Quick mask mode

Painting with white

Resulting selection

Painting with black

Resulting selection

Lesson 8: Finished artwork

8-1: Clipping Groups

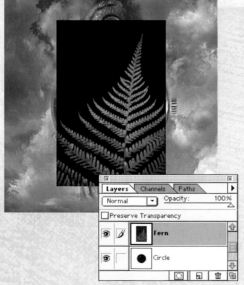

Before clipping fern to circle   *Result of clipping fern to circle*

8-2: Clipping an adjustment layer

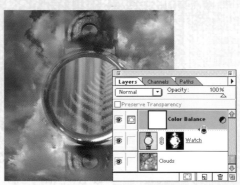

*Color Balance adjustment layer affecting
lower layers*

*Color Balance adjustment layer grouped with
watch layer*

8-3: Adjustment layer masks

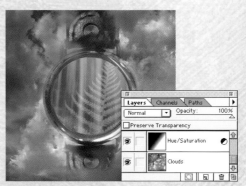

Hue/Saturation adjustment layer

*Hue/Saturation adjustment layer containing
gradient*

Project B: Finished artwork

B-1: Photoshop color wheel

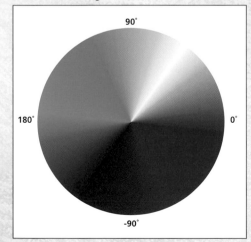

Colorize option set to 90° on color wheel

Colorize option set to -56° on color wheel

Lesson 9: Finished artwork

10-1: Looking at tonal range

Image with sufficient tonal range

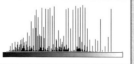

Image with insufficient tonal range

10-2: Average-key image and histogram

10-3: Low-key image and histogram

10-4: High-key image and histogram

10-5: Tonal correction using Brightness/Contrast

Before

After

10-6: Tonal correction using Auto Levels

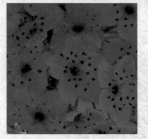

Before

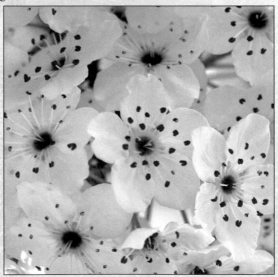

After

10-7: Tonal correction using Levels

Before

After

10-8: Tonal correction using black and white point settings

Before

After

10-9: Tonal correction using Curves

Before

After

10-10: Tonal correction using Color Balance

Before

After

Project C: Uncorrected artwork

Project C: Finished artwork

Lesson 11: Finished artwork

11-1: Clipping path exported with image to page layout program

11-2: JPEG Compression

Quality maximum

Quality low

Soft-edged original image

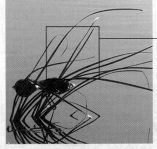

Quality maximum

Quality low

Hard-edged original image

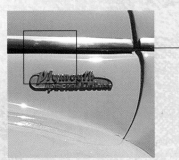

Quality maximum

Quality low

Original image containing both soft and hard edges

Lesson 12: Finished artwork

12-1: Comparing file size and image quality of GIF files

256 colors, 128K

64 colors, 64K

8 colors, 32K

Lesson 13: Finished artwork

13-1: RGB image with red, green, and blue channels

 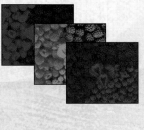 

13-2: CMYK image with cyan, magenta, yellow and black channels

 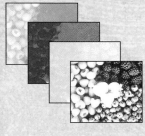

D-1: Duotone samples

Original image

Duotone: Cyan bl 2

Duotone: Magenta bl 3

Duotone: Yellow bl 2

Tritone: Bmt brown 1

Tritone: Bcy green 1

*Quadtone: CMYK
ext wm*

*Tritone: CMYK very
cool*

Duotone Adjustments

Identical tritone curves, different ink colors

Different tritone curves, identical ink colors

8

Lesson 8

Advanced Layer Techniques

Once you've learned basic layer techniques, you can begin to create more complex effects in your artwork using layer masks, clipping groups, and adjustment layers. Layer masks let you hide or reveal parts of the artwork on a layer. Clipping groups let you define an object on one layer as a mask for artwork on another layer. Adjustment layers let you apply global or selective effects that can be edited repeatedly without making a permanent change to the pixels in the image.

In this lesson, you'll learn how to do the following:

• Create and edit layer masks to selectively hide and reveal portions of artwork on a layer.

• Add guides to an image to precisely align parts of the image.

• Create clipping groups, which let you use an image on one layer as a mask for artwork on another layer.

• Add adjustment layers to an image to make global adjustments and selective adjustments to an image.

• Use the Preserve Transparency option to affect only the areas of a layer that contain pixel values, thereby preserving the transparency of the blank areas of a layer.

• Add a drop shadow to an image.

• Delete a layer mask.

• Save layered files.

Restoring default preferences

Before starting this lesson, delete the Adobe Photoshop Preferences file to restore the program's default palettes and command settings. For step-by-step instructions about how to delete the preferences file, see "Restoring default preferences" on page 4.

Restart Adobe Photoshop.

Getting started

Before you begin working, you'll open the finished artwork to get an idea of what you'll create.

1 Choose File > Open. Locate and open the Lesson08 folder; then select End08.psd and click Open.

A photo collage of a watch suspended in clouds appears.

2 If desired, choose View > Zoom Out to make the image smaller and leave it on your screen as you work. If you don't want to leave the image open, choose File > Close.

You'll start this lesson by opening an image that contains two layers, and then you'll work with various layering and masking techniques to complete the image.

3 Choose File > Open, locate and select Start08.psd in the Lesson08 folder, and then click Open.

4 Choose File > Save As, enter the name Work08.psd, and click Save.

In the Layers palette, notice that there are two layers in the document—the Watch layer and the Clouds layer. At this point, you can see only the Watch layer, because the Clouds layer is positioned under the watch.

5 In the Layers palette, click the eye icon next to the Watch layer to hide it; the clouds on the layer beneath the Watch layer are revealed. Make the Watch layer visible before continuing to the next step.

Working with layer masks

Layer masks let you hide or reveal portions of the artwork on an individual layer. You can control how much of the artwork is hidden or revealed by painting on the mask using black, white, or a shade of gray.

Where you paint with black, the mask is completely opaque, hiding the artwork on the layer. Where you paint with white, the mask is completely transparent, revealing the artwork on the layer. Where you paint with a shade of gray, the mask is semitransparent, making the artwork on the layer partially transparent.

You'll start by adding a layer mask to the Watch layer. You will paint on the layer mask to hide and reveal portions of the watch, letting the clouds on the underlying layer show through.

1 In the Layers palette, click the Watch layer to make it the active layer.

2 Select the lasso tool ($\wp$) in the toolbox; then drag a loose selection around the watch, including a portion of the watchband.

3 Choose Select > Feather, enter 25 in the Feather Radius text box, and then click OK. Adding a feather radius to the selection will soften the edges of the selected area when you add the layer mask.

4 Choose Layer > Add Layer Mask > Reveal Selection. The Reveal Selection option displays the selected portion of the watch and makes the unselected areas on the Watch layer transparent.

In the Layers palette, a layer mask thumbnail appears to the right of the layer thumbnail of the watch, indicating that a layer mask has been added.

Two additional icons appear when you create a layer mask—a small square with a dotted circle appears in the column next to the eye icon, indicating that the layer mask is selected; and a link icon appears between the layer thumbnail and the layer mask thumbnail to indicate that the layer and the mask are linked.

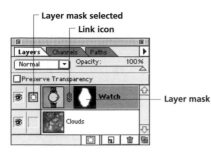

Layer mask selected
Link icon
Layer mask

5 Choose File > Save to save your work.

Painting on a layer mask

Now you will paint on the mask using black, white, and a shade of gray to hide, reveal, and partially reveal the clouds on the underlying layer. As a reminder, painting with black hides the artwork on the layer, painting with white reveals the artwork on the layer, and painting with a shade of gray makes the artwork on the layer partially transparent.

1 In the Layers palette, click the layer mask thumbnail on the Watch layer to make sure that the layer mask is selected.

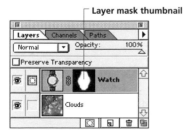

Layer mask thumbnail

2 Make sure that black is the foreground color and white is the background color.

3 Choose File > Preferences > Display & Cursors. In the Painting Cursors section of the dialog box, select the Brush Size option and click OK.

4 Select the paintbrush tool ( ) in the toolbox; then click the Brushes palette tab and select a large, soft-edged brush.

You'll start by painting with black to hide part of the watchband and some of the watch.

5 Begin painting on the watchband and along the outside edge of the watch. (Don't be too careful here.)

As you paint with black, the area surrounding the watch is hidden (revealing more of the clouds on the underlying layer). In the Layers palette, notice how the layer mask is altered as you paint.

Now you'll paint with white to reveal more of the watch and the watchband.

6 Click the Switch Colors icon in the toolbox to swap the foreground and background colors. White becomes the foreground color.

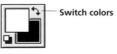

Switch colors

Press *x* on the keyboard to switch the foreground and background colors.

7 Begin painting with white where the clouds cover the border of the watch, and paint to reveal a bit more of the watchband. Notice how the layer mask layer thumbnail is updated in the Layers palette.

Now that you've experimented using black and white to hide and reveal the artwork on the layer, you'll paint with a shade of gray to partially reveal some of the watch.

8 Click the Swatches palette tab to bring the palette to the front of its group; then select a medium-gray color.

Note: Although you are working with an RGB image, only shades of gray are displayed in the Swatches palette when editing a layer mask.

9 Begin painting over a portion of the watch border and a small area along a part of the watch face.

As you paint, you'll notice that the watch becomes partially visible, letting you see part of the watch and part of the clouds. (The lighter the shade of gray you paint with, the more the clouds are revealed.)

10 Choose File > Save to save your work.

Unlinking layer masks

By default, layer masks are linked to the artwork on the layer. When you move a mask or the artwork, both the mask and the artwork are repositioned. You can unlink the layer mask and the artwork on the layer if you want to move them independently.

1 In the Layers palette, click the link icon between the layer thumbnail and the layer mask thumbnail to turn off linking.

Linking off

2 In the Layers palette, click the watch thumbnail in the Watch layer.

3 Select the move tool (⊹) in the toolbox and drag in the image window to move the artwork. Notice that the layer mask thumbnail does not move with the artwork.

Moving the artwork on the layer

4 Choose Edit > Undo to undo the move.

5 Now click the layer mask thumbnail and drag the move tool to move the layer mask. The layer mask moves independently of the layer mask.

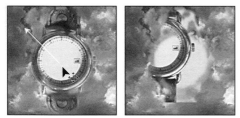

6 Choose Edit > Undo to undo the move.

7 Click the area between the layer thumbnail and the layer mask thumbnail to relink the layer mask and the artwork.

You can also turn off a layer mask to view the artwork on the layer without the mask.

8 To turn off the layer mask, Shift-click the layer mask thumbnail on the Watch layer in the Layers palette. A large red *x* appears on the layer mask thumbnail.

9 To turn on the layer mask, click the layer mask thumbnail in the Layers palette. The *x* disappears.

10 Choose File > Revert to return to the last saved version of the file.

Adding guides to align artwork

Guides help you align artwork in an image. To create a guide, you turn on the rulers and then drag from the horizontal or vertical ruler. You'll add guides to the Watch image to assist you in finding the center point of the image.

1 Choose View > Show Rulers. The default unit of measurement for the rulers is inches. You'll notice that this image is 6 inches by 6 inches.

Note: To change the unit of measurement for the rulers, choose File > Preferences > Units and Rulers, and then select the desired unit of measurement from the Units menu.

2 Position the pointer anywhere within the horizontal ruler at the top of the image, and then drag downward to align a guide at the 3-inch mark on the vertical ruler. Release the mouse button to place the guide.

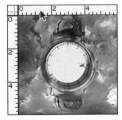 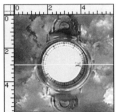

Positioning pointer in ruler *Dragging a guide into the image window*

3 Position the pointer anywhere within the vertical ruler at the left side of the image, and then drag to the right to align a guide at the 3-inch mark on the horizontal ruler. Release the mouse button to place the guide.

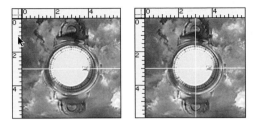

Note: If you need to reposition a guide, click the move tool in the toolbox, position the move tool on the guide, and then drag to reposition the guide.

Next, you'll create a new layer and use the guides to align a circle you'll draw. (You'll use the circle to enhance the artwork in a few minutes.)

4 In the Layers palette, make sure that the Watch layer is selected, and then click the New Layer button at the bottom of the palette.

5 Double-click the new layer, enter the name Circle in the Layer Options dialog box, and then click OK. The Circle layer should be at the top of the Layers palette.

6 Select the ellipse marquee tool (⬭) from the hidden tools palette under the rectangle marquee.

7 Position the crosshair at the intersection of the guides, hold down Option+Shift (Macintosh) or Alt+Shift (Windows), and then drag from the center point to the inside edge of the watch face. Release the mouse button; then release the modifier keys.

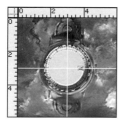

Holding down Option (Macintosh) or Alt (Windows) draws the circle from the center point, and Shift constrains the selection marquee to a circle.

Now you'll fill the circle with black.

8 Make sure that the foreground and background colors are set to black and white.

🔆 Press *d* on the keyboard to return to the default foreground and background colors.

9 Choose Edit > Fill. Make sure that Foreground is selected and that the opacity is set to 100%; then click OK to fill the circle with black.

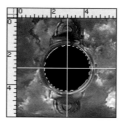

10 Choose Select > None to deselect everything.

11 Choose View > Hide Guides to turn off the guides while you continue to work.

12 Choose File > Save to save your work.

Creating a clipping group

You can mask an object on one layer using an image from another layer by creating a *clipping group*. In a clipping group, the bottom, or *base layer*, of the group controls the shape, opacity, and mode of any successive layers. (You can also set opacity levels and modes for individual layers.) The layer or layers above the base layer are clipped to (or masked by) the shape of the object or objects on the base layer.

You'll use the circle you drew as the base layer of a clipping group. See illustration 8–1 in the color section of this book for a sample of a clipping group.

1 In the Lesson08 folder, locate and select the Fern.psd file, and click Open.

You'll move the fern image onto the New-watch.psd window and then clip the fern to the circle.

2 If necessary, reposition both windows so that you can see a part of each of them. Then click the Fern window to make it the active window.

3 In the Layers palette, hold down Shift and drag the Fern layer onto the Work08.psd image.

Holding down Shift as you drag centers the fern in the Work08 window. The Fern layer should now be positioned at the top of the Layers palette in the Work08.psd window.

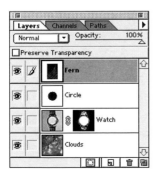

The next step is to clip the fern to the Circle layer. (In effect, you'll be masking the fern with the circular shape.)

4 With the Fern layer selected in the Layers palette, choose Layer > Group with Previous. The fern is clipped to the circle.

In the Layers palette, the base layer in the clipping group (the circle) is underlined, and any layers above the base layer that are part of the clipping group (the fern) are indented.

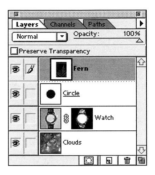

5 If you want to adjust the position of the fern within the circle, click the move tool in the toolbox and drag.

Next, you'll add another image to the clipping group.

6 In the Lesson08 folder, locate and select the Waterfal.psd file, and click Open. If necessary, reposition both windows so that you can see a part of each of them.

7 In the Layers palette, hold down Shift and drag the Waterfall layer onto the New-watch.psd image.

The Waterfall layer should be positioned at the top of the Layers palette in the Newwatch.psd window.

You can make adjustments to each individual layer in a clipping group. You'll change the mode and opacity of the waterfall before adding it to the clipping group.

8 In the Layers palette, drag the Opacity slider to 80% (or type 8 on the keypad), and for mode choose Screen. You'll be able to see through the waterfall.

This time, you'll try a keyboard shortcut to add the waterfall to the clipping group.

9 In the Layers palette, hold down Option (Macintosh) or Alt (Windows), position the pointer on the line between the waterfall layer and the circle layer, and then click to add the waterfall to the clipping group.

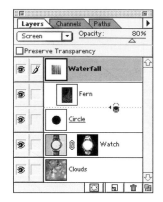

10 Close the Fern.psd image and the Waterfal.psd images, and do not save changes.

Adding adjustment layers

Adjustment layers can be added to an image to apply global effects without permanently changing the pixel values in the image. For example, if you add a Hue/Saturation adjustment layer to an image, you can experiment with different colors repeatedly, because the change occurs only on the adjustment layer. If you decide to return to the original pixel values, you can hide or delete the adjustment layer.

You will add a Hue/Saturation adjustment layer to the Work08 image, and then add the adjustment layer to the clipping group.

1 In the Layers palette, make sure that the Waterfall layer is selected, and then choose Layer > New > Adjustment Layer.

💡 Hold down Command (Macintosh) or Ctrl (Windows) and click the New Layer button in the Layers palette to create a new adjustment layer.

2 In the Adjustment Layer dialog box, for Type choose Hue/Saturation, and then click OK.

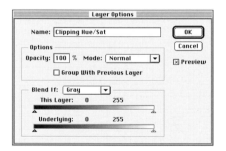

3 In the Hue/Saturation dialog box, select the Colorize option to set all the values to 0° on the color wheel, which is red.

See illustration B-1 in the color section of this book to see how colors are arranged on the color wheel.

The Colorize option differs from the Hue/Saturation options, which change pixels based on their existing color values in the image.

4 Using the sliders or by making entries in the text boxes, enter **93** for hue, **13** for saturation, and **0** for the lightness.

5 Click OK; the Hue/Saturation adjustment layer is added above the Waterfall layer in the Layers palette.

Adjustment layers are automatically named and don't display thumbnail previews; only the layer mask thumbnail is displayed. You can also rename adjustment layers, which can be helpful if you want to add more than one adjustment layer of the same kind.

6 Make sure that the Hue/Saturation adjustment layer is selected in the Layers palette; then choose Layer > Layer Options.

7 Rename the adjustment layer **Clipping Hue/Sat**, and click OK.

8 If you're not satisfied with your results, double-click the Clipping Hue/Sat layer in the Layers palette, and select new settings for the hue, saturation, and lightness.

At this point, the Clipping Hue/Sat adjustment layer affects all the layers in the image. You'll add the adjustment layer to the clipping group so that only the layers in the clipping group will be affected by the adjustment layer.

9 In the Layers palette, position the pointer on the line that separates the Hue/Saturation layer and the Waterfall layer; then hold down Option (Macintosh) or Alt (Windows) and click the line.

10 Choose File > Save to save your work.

You'll add another adjustment layer above the watch to adjust the color of just the watch. This time, you'll turn off all the layers except the watch layer and the clouds layer so you can see precisely what happens when you add the adjustment layer.

11 Before you begin, click the Size box (Macintosh) or Maximize box (Windows) in the top right corner of the Layers palette to make sure that you can see all the layers in the image.

12 In the Layers palette, click the Watch layer to make it the active layer. Then drag through the eye column to turn off all layers but the Watch layer and the Clouds layer.

13 Choose Layer > New > Adjustment Layer.

14 In the Adjustment Layer dialog box, for Type select Color Balance, and click OK.

15 In the Color Balance dialog box, make sure that the Preview option is selected and then use the text boxes (from left to right) or the sliders to enter these values: 31, 0, –56. Accept the remainder of the settings, and click OK.

The preview shows the color adjustment applied to the Watch layer and any layers below it.

16 Choose Layer > Group with Previous to clip the adjustment layer to only the Watch layer.

See illustration 8–2 in the color section of this book for a sample of an adjustment layer used in a clipping group.

17 In the Layers palette, drag through the eye column to turn on all the layers.

18 In the Layers palette, select the Clouds layer.

19 Choose Layer > New > Adjustment Layer; select Hue/Saturation from the Type menu, and click OK.

20 Click the Colorize option, and then drag the sliders until you've selected a color you like. Click OK. The adjustment layer is added to the Layers palette above the Clouds layer.

The hue you selected is applied to the entire Clouds layer. You'll add a gradient to the Hue/Saturation adjustment layer to reveal the color gradually across the image.

21 Double-click the gradient tool in the toolbox. In the Gradient Tool Options palette, for Type select Black, White.

22 With the Hue/Saturation layer selected in the Layers palette, drag diagonally from the top left area to the lower right area of the watch face.

Note: Although you're dragging in the image window, the gradient is actually being applied only to the layer mask on the adjustment layer.

When you release the mouse button, the gradient is applied to the adjustment layer. As the gradient moves from white to black, the color is revealed gradually over the length of the gradient. See illustration 8–3 for a sample of a mask applied to an adjustment layer.

23 Choose File > Save to save your work.

Adding a drop shadow

You'll add a face to the watch and then create a drop shadow behind the watch face to add depth to the image.

1 In the Layers palette, select the Clipping Hue/Sat adjustment layer.

1 Choose File > Open. Locate and open the Lesson08 folder; then select Face.psd and click Open.

2 Hold down Shift, and drag the Face layer from the Layers palette into the New-watch.psd window. The Face layer is added at the top of the Layers palette.

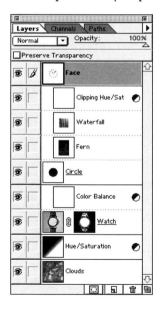

3 Close the Face.psd file before continuing.

Creating a drop shadow is a simple task when using layers. All you have to do is duplicate and paint a copy of the original layer, and then reposition the copy behind the original layer.

4 Drag the Face layer onto the New Layer button at the bottom of the Layers palette to duplicate the Face layer.

5 With the Face copy layer active, click the Preserve Transparency option.

With the Preserve Transparency option turned on, you don't have to make a selection before you paint; only the areas where pixel values already exist are affected when you paint.

```
Layers   Channels   Paths         ►
Normal      ▼   Opacity:      100%
☒ Preserve Transparency
👁  ✏️   ⌚   Face copy
👁      ⌚   Face
```

Now, you'll paint the drop shadow numbers white.

6 Make sure that the foreground and background colors are set to the defaults.

7 Hold down Command (Macintosh) or Ctrl (Windows), and press Delete. The hands are filled with the background color, which is white.

8 Hold down Command/Ctrl to select the move tool from the keyboard; then press the right arrow key twice and the down arrow key twice to reposition the white numbers.

9 In the Layers palette, drag the Face copy layer below the Face layer to reposition the layer. Voila! You've created a drop shadow.

Lightening and darkening areas of an image

The dodge and burn tools let you lighten and darken areas of an image selectively. You'll add highlights to the watch face using these tools.

1 Select the dodge tool (🔍) in the toolbox.

2 In the Brushes palette, select a soft-edged brush from the second row of brushes.

3 In the Layers palette, click the Waterfall layer to make it the active layer; then drag a curved stroke in the upper left quadrant of the watch face. As you drag, the area becomes lighter.

You can hold down the mouse button and drag repeatedly over the same area lighten the area more, or you can use short single strokes to lighten the area incrementally.

4 Select the burn tool (☜) tool in the hidden tools palette under the dodge tool.

5 Drag the burn tool over the lower right quadrant of the watch face to darken the area.

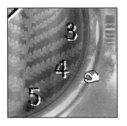

Removing layer masks

Each layer mask in a file increases the file's size. To minimize the size of your files, it's important to remove or merge layer masks after you've made final design decisions.

You'll merge the layer mask on the Watch layer with the artwork on the layer.

1 In the Layers palette, select the Watch layer.

2 Choose Layer > Remove Layer Mask.

3 When the prompt appears, click Apply to merge the layer mask with the artwork on the layer.

4 Choose File > Save to save your work.

Flattening a layered image

If you plan to send your documents out for proofs, it's a good idea to save two versions of your file—one containing all the layers

and layer masks so that you can edit the file if necessary, and one flattened version to send to your print shop.

1 First, note the file size in the lower left corner of the Work08.psd image.

2 Choose Image > Duplicate, name the duplicate file Final08.psd, and click OK.

3 Choose Flatten Image from the Layers palette menu. The Final08.psd file is combined onto a single background.

4 Now check the file size of the Final08.psd image. You'll notice that it is significantly smaller than the Work08.psd image, because it has been flattened onto the background.

You've completed the Advanced Layers lesson. Experiment with your own work to see how you can use layer masks and adjustment layers.

Review
• What happens when you paint with black on a layer mask? With white? With gray?

• How do you turn off a layer mask to view only the artwork on the layer?

• What is a clipping group? Can you think of how you might use it in your own work?

• How do adjustment layers work, and what is the benefit of using an adjustment layer?

• How do you rename an adjustment layer, and why would you want to?

• What does an adjustment layer affect when it is added to a clipping group?

B

Project B
Creating Special Effects

The huge assortment of filters in Adobe Photoshop lets you transform ordinary images into extraordinary digital artwork. You can select filters that simulate a traditional artistic medium—for example, a watercolor, pastel, or sketched effect—or you can choose from filters that blur, bend, wrap, sharpen, or fragment images. In addition to using filters to alter images, you can use adjustment layers and painting modes to vary the look of your artwork.

This project shows you how to do the following:

• Add a grid to an image to help you make precise selections.

• Desaturate a selection without affecting the color in other parts of the image.

• Paint on a layer above the artwork to color the underlying artwork without changing it permanently.

• Add an adjustment layer to make a color correction to a selection.

• Apply filters to selections to create a variety of effects.

Restoring default preferences

Before starting this lesson, delete the Adobe Photoshop Preferences file to restore the program's default palettes and command settings. For step-by-step instructions, see "Restoring default preferences" on page 4.

Restart Adobe Photoshop.

Getting started

Before you begin working, you'll open the finished art to get an idea of what you'll create.

1 Choose File > Open. Locate and open the ProjectB folder, then select EndB.psd and click Open.

An image containing six sets of pears appears. Some of the pears have been painted, and some have had filters applied to them.

2 If desired, choose View > Zoom Out to make the image smaller and leave it on your screen as you work. If you don't want to leave the image open, choose File > Close.

Now you'll open the start file and begin working.

3 Choose File > Open. Locate and open the ProjectB folder, then select StartB.psd and click Open.

4 Choose File > Save As, enter the name Work08b.psd, and click Save.

Desaturating a selection

To begin the project, you'll desaturate a selection, add a layer, and then hand-color it.

You'll start by displaying a grid and using it to help you make a precise selection. A grid helps you lay out images or elements symmetrically. Selections, selection borders, and tools snap to the grid when they are dragged within 8 screen pixels of it.

1 Choose View > Show Grid. The grid with the default settings appears in the image window.

2 Choose File > Preferences > Guides & Grid.

You adjust the grid settings using the Preferences dialog box. You can set the grid to display as lines or as points, and you can change its spacing or color.

3 In the Grid section of the dialog box, for Color, choose Green. For Gridline Every, enter a value of 2; for Subdivisions, enter a value of 1. Click OK to apply the changes to the grid.

4 Select the zoom tool (Q) in the toolbox, and zoom in on the pear image in the top left corner of the file.

5 Using the rectangle marquee tool ([ ]), drag a marquee to select the top left set of pears. As you drag, the marquee snaps to the grid.

Next, you'll use the Desaturate command to *desaturate*, or remove the color, from the pear selection. Saturation is the presence or absence of color in a selection. When you desaturate a selection within an image, you create a grayscale-like effect without affecting the colors in other parts of the image.

6 Choose Image > Adjust > Desaturate. The color is removed from the selection.

7 Choose Select > None.

8 Choose File > Save to save your work.

Applying painting effects

Now you'll paint the pears using a combination of colors and painting blending modes. To color the selection without making a permanent change, you'll add a layer above the pears and paint on the layer. This way, if you don't like the results, you can simply erase the layer and start over.

1 In the Layers palette, click the New Layer button to add Layer 1 to the image.

2 In the Layers palette, double-click Layer 1, rename the layer Paint, and click OK. Using the pop-up menu to the left of the Opacity slider, choose Color for mode.

The Color mode lets you change the hue of a selection without affecting the highlights and shadows, making it a useful mode for applying color tints to a selection.

3 Select the lasso tool (⊘) in the toolbox, and then draw a selection around the right pear so you can confine painting to that area. If necessary, add to the selection using Shift, or subtract from the selection using Option (Macintosh) or Alt (Windows), and redraw the selection.

4 Save the selection of the right pear by choosing Select > Save Selection, and click OK to save the selection in a new channel (#4 by default). You'll use the selection again for another sets of pears.

5 Double-click the paintbrush tool (✏) in the toolbox.

6 In the Paintbrush Options palette, set the Opacity to about 50%.

💡 Change the paintbrush opacity by pressing a number on the keypad from 1 to 9 (where 1 is 10%, 9 is 90%, and 0 is 100%).

7 Click the Brushes palette tab; then select a large, soft-edged brush.

8 In the Swatches palette, click a yellow-green color that appeals to you for the foreground color.

9 Paint the entire pear with the light yellow-green color. As you paint, you'll notice that the color of the pear changes to the color you selected.

10 Next, select a darker green from the Swatches palette. In the Paintbrush Options palette, set the brush opacity to about 30%.

11 Continue painting around the edges in the pear selection, avoiding the highlight area.

12 To add additional highlights to the pear, select a rose color from the Swatches palette, and select a smaller brush from the Brushes palette. In the Paintbrush Options palette, use the slider to decrease the paint opacity to about 20%, and paint more highlights on the pear.

13 Choose Select > None.

14 Choose File > Save to save your work.

Now you'll add a gradient to the other pear for a highlight effect.

15 Select the left pear using the lasso tool.

16 Choose Select > Save Selection, and click OK to save the selection of the left pear in a new channel (#5 by default). You'll use this selection again for other sets of pears.

17 In the Color palette, select red as the foreground color.

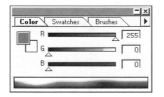

18 Click the background color swatch, and select yellow as the background color.

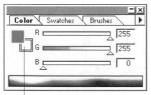
└ **Select background swatch**

19 Double-click the gradient tool (▒▓) in the toolbox. In the Gradient Options palette, choose Radial for Type, and set the opacity to 40%.

20 Position the gradient tool on the highlight of the pear, and drag toward the stem. (You can drag the gradient tool in different directions to try out different effects.)

21 Choose Select > None.

22 When you've finished painting the set of pears, choose Layer > Merge Visible to merge the painting layer with the pear image and to keep the file size small. You'll continue the project by applying effects to the other pears in the image.

23 Choose File > Save to save your work.

Loading a selection

You can load saved selections and reuse them. You'll select the middle pears by loading and combining the individual selections you saved earlier.

1 Select the zoom tool from the toolbox; then hold down Option (Macintosh) or Alt (Windows) to select the zoom-out tool (⊖).

2 Click the zoom-out tool as many times as necessary until both the top left pears and top middle pears are visible.

3 Choose Select > Load Selection, and select Channel #4. Click OK.

4 Choose Select > Load Selection. Select Channel #5, and click Add to Selection. Click OK. Now both pears are selected.

5 Using the marquee tool (▢), drag the selection to the right to position it over the middle pears in the top row.

Colorizing a selection

You can tint a selection a solid shade using the Colorize option. When you select the Colorize option in the Hue/Saturation dialog box, all the colors in the selection are reset to the 0∞ point on the color wheel

(red), which differs from the default methods of changing the hue and saturation of pixels based on their existing values.

To see how the colors are arranged on the color wheel, see illustration B–1 in the color section of this book.

1 Double-click the hand tool (✋) in the toolbox to fit the image in the window. The top middle pears should still be selected.

2 Choose Image > Adjust > Hue/Saturation. Select the Colorize option.

3 Enter **83** in the Hue text box, and **28** in the Saturation text box.

The image takes on a greenish tint, because the Hue value of 50 is located 50° counterclockwise from red (0∞) on the color wheel. Decreasing the saturation lowers the intensity of the color.

4 Click OK to apply the changes.

5 To preview the changes without the selection marquee, choose View > Hide Edges.

6 Choose View > Show Edges, and then choose Select > None to deselect everything.

7 Choose File > Save to save your work.

Changing the color balance

Next you'll set the rectangle marquee tool to a fixed size to make subsequent selections easier, and then add an adjustment layer to a selection to change the color balance in the image. By applying an adjustment layer to a selection, you can edit the colors as many times as you like without making the changes permanent.

1 Select the rectangle marquee tool (⬚) in the toolbox, and then drag a selection marquee over the pears in the top right corner of the image.

2 Choose View > Hide Grid to hide the grid.

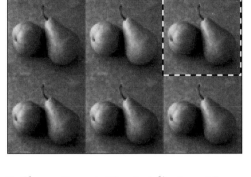

3 Choose Layer > New > Adjustment Layer. For Type, choose Color Balance and click OK.

4 In the Color Balance dialog box, enter the following values: **+13, −14** and **−38.** Click OK.

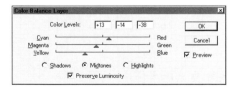

Notice that the adjustment layer thumbnail in the Layers palette resembles a mask. By making a selection and then adding an

adjustment layer, the layer becomes a mask that applies the adjustment only to the selected area.

Adjustment layers act as layer masks, which can be edited repeatedly without permanently affecting the underlying image. You can double-click an adjustment layer to display the last settings used, and adjust them repeatedly, or you can delete an adjustment layer by dragging it to the Trash button at the bottom of the Layers palette.

5 Choose File > Save to save your work.

Applying filters

To conclude the project, you'll apply different styles of filters to the remaining pears. Because Adobe Photoshop includes so many different filters for creating special effects, the best way to learn about them is to try out different filters and filter options.

1 In the Layers palette, select the background.

2 Using the rectangle marquee tool (⬚), drag the selection marquee over the pears in the lower left corner of the image.

3 Choose Filter > Brush Strokes > Cross-hatch. Adjust the settings as desired, using the Preview window to see the effect. Click OK.

You can fade the effect of a filter or of a color adjustment using the Fade command. The mode determines how the modified pixels in the selection appear in relation to the original pixels. The blending modes in the Fade dialog box are a subset of those available in the painting and editing tools Options palette.

4 Choose Filter > Fade Crosshatch to fade the filter effect. For mode, choose Multiply. Set the Opacity to 50% and click OK.

5 Using the rectangle marquee tool, drag the selection marquee to select the middle set of pears in the bottom row of the image.

6 Choose Filter > Distort > Zigzag. For Amount, enter **4%**; for Ridges, enter **9%**; for style, select Pond Ripples. Click OK. The

Zigzag filter distorts an image radially, creating ripples or ridges in an image.

7 Using the rectangle marquee tool, select the pears in the lower right corner of the bottom row.

8 Click the Default Colors icon in the toolbox to set the foreground and background colors to their defaults.

9 Choose Filter > Distort > Diffuse Glow. For Graininess, enter **6**; for Glow Amount, enter **6**; and for Clear Amount, select **15**. Click OK. This filter adds white noise (pixels) to an image.

10 Choose File > Save to save your work; then close the file.

This concludes the Special Effects project. Try out other filters to see how you can add a variety of effects to your images.

9

Lesson 9

Basic Pen Tool Techniques

The pen tool draws precise straight or curved lines called paths. You can use the pen tool as a drawing tool or as a selection tool. When used as a selection tool, the pen tool always draws smooth, anti-aliased outlines. These paths are an excellent alternative to using the standard selection tools for creating intricate selections.

In this lesson, you'll learn how to do the following:

• Practice drawing straight and curved paths using the pen tool.

• Save paths.

• Fill and stroke paths.

• Edit paths using the path editing tools.

• Convert a path to a selection.

• Convert a selection to a path.

Restoring default preferences

Before starting this lesson, delete the Adobe Photoshop Preferences file to restore the program's default palettes and command settings. For step-by-step instructions about how to delete the preferences file, see "Restoring default preferences" on page 4.

Restart Adobe Photoshop.

Opening the work file

You'll begin by working with templates that guide you through the process of creating straight paths, curved paths, and paths that are a combination of both. In addition, you'll learn how to add points to a path, how to subtract points from a path, and how to convert a straight line to a curve and vice versa. After you've practiced drawing and editing paths using the templates, you'll open an image and practice drawing a path.

Choose File > Open. Locate and open the Lesson09 folder; then select Straight.psd and click Open.

An image containing a template of straight lines appears. You'll practice drawing straight paths using a template, so that you can practice drawing the paths as many times as you like.

Drawing paths with the pen tool

The pen tool draws straight and curved lines called *paths*, which may be open paths or closed paths. Open paths are paths with two distinct endpoints. Closed paths are continuous; for example, a circle is a closed path. Paths do not print when you print your artwork.

1 Click the pen tool (◊) in the toolbox.

Press *p* on the keyboard to select the pen tool.

2 Click the Paths palette tab to bring the palette to the front of its group. The Paths palette displays thumbnail previews of the paths you draw.

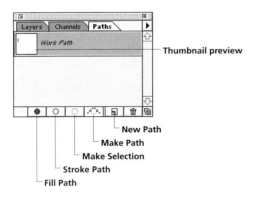

— Thumbnail preview

— New Path
— Make Path
— Make Selection
— Stroke Path
— Fill Path

Drawing straight paths

Straight paths are created by clicking the mouse button. The first time you click the mouse button, you set a starting point for a path. Each time thereafter that you click the mouse, a straight line is drawn between the previous point and the current point.

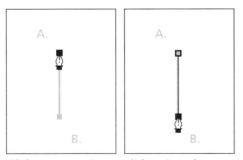

Click to set a starting point…   *click again to draw a straight line.*

1 Position the pen tool on point A and click the pen tool; then click point B to create a straight line path.

As you draw paths, a temporary storage area named Work Path appears in the Paths palette to keep track of the paths you draw.

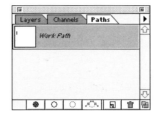

2 End the path by clicking the pen tool in the toolbox.

The points that connect paths are called *anchor points.* You can drag individual anchor points to edit segments of a path, or you can select all the anchor points to select the entire path.

You'll learn more about anchor points later in this lesson.

3 Double-click the Work Path in the Paths palette to open the Save Path dialog box. Type the name **Straight Lines** and click OK to rename the path. The path is selected in the Paths palette.

4 Select the arrow tool (↖) from the hidden tools palette under the pen tool.

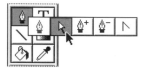

💡 Press *p* repeatedly to scroll through all the hidden tools under the pen tool.

5 Click the path in the window to select it, and then move the path by dragging anywhere on the path using the arrow tool.

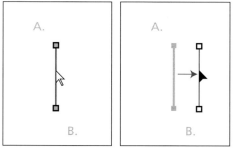

Selecting a path   *Moving a path*

6 To adjust the angle or length of the path, drag one of the anchor points with the arrow tool.

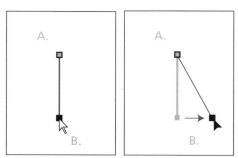

Adjusting the path angle

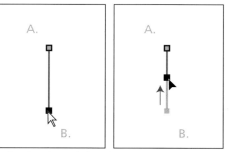

Adjusting the path length

7 Select the pen tool in the hidden tools palette in the toolbox (right now it's under the arrow tool).

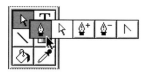

8 To begin the next path, click point C with the pen tool. Notice that an *x* appears in the Paths palette to indicate that you are starting a new path.

9 Click point D to draw a path between the two points.

10 End the path using either of the following methods:

• Click the pen tool in the toolbox.

• Hold down Command (Macintosh) or Ctrl (Windows), and click away from the path. Holding down Command/Ctrl while the pen tool is active selects the arrow tool.

11 Click point E to begin the next path; then hold down Shift and click points F, G, H, and I. Holding down Shift as you click the subsequent points constrains the path to a 45∞ angle.

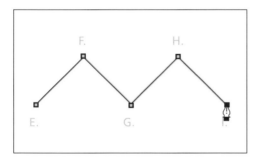

If you make a mistake while you're drawing, choose Edit > Undo to undo the last anchor point; then click the pen tool to continue.

12 End the path using one of the methods you've learned.

When a path contains more than one segment, you can drag individual anchor points to adjust individual segments of the path. You can also select all the anchor points in a path to edit the entire path.

13 Select the arrow tool from the hidden tools palette under the pen tool.

14 Try dragging individual anchor points to move segments of the zigzag path you just drew.

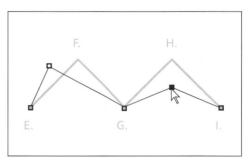

15 To select an entire path, Option-click (Macintosh) or Alt-click (Windows) with the arrow tool. When an entire path is selected, all the anchor points are solid.

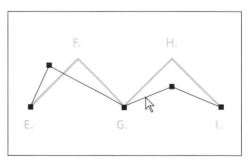

16 Drag the path to move the entire path; then choose Edit > Undo to undo the move.

Next, you'll draw a closed path.

17 Select the pen tool from the toolbox.

18 Click point J to begin the path; then click point K and point L.

When you position the pen tool over the starting point to end the path, a small circle appears with the pen tool to indicate that the path will be closed when you click.

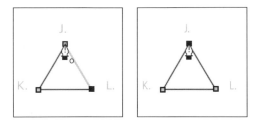

19 To close the path, position the pointer over the starting point (point J) and click.

When you close a path, you don't have to click the pen tool to end the path; closing the path ends the path.

If desired, practice drawing another closed path using the star shape on the template as a guide.

At this point, all of the paths you've drawn appear in the Straight Lines path in the Paths Palette. Each individual path on the Straight Lines path is called a *subpath*.

Painting paths

You can fill or stroke the paths and subpaths you draw. To fill or stroke a path, you must first select it.

1 Select the arrow tool (⬉) in the hidden tools palette under the pen tool.

2 In the image window, click the zigzag line with the arrow tool to select it; then choose Stroke Subpath from the Paths palette menu.

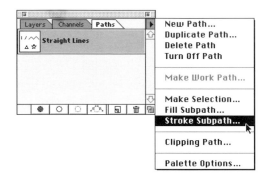

3 For Tool, choose Airbrush and click OK. The path is stroked with the current airbrush settings.

Note: You can select a painting tool and set attributes before you select the tool in the Stroke Subpath dialog box.

Now try filling one of the paths.

4 Click the triangular closed path with the arrow tool; then choose Fill Subpath from the Paths palette menu. The Fill dialog box appears.

5 Click OK to accept the defaults. The triangular path is filled with the foreground color.

6 To hide the paths, click below the path names in the blank area of the Paths palette.

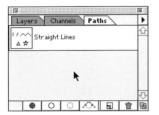

7 Choose File > Close, and do not save changes.

Drawing curved paths

Curved paths are created by clicking and dragging the mouse button. The first time you click and drag the mouse, you set a starting point for the curved path and also determine the direction of the curve. Each time thereafter that you drag the mouse, a curved path is drawn between the previous point and the current point.

As you drag the pen tool, Photoshop draws *direction lines* and *direction points* from the anchor point. Direction lines and points are used to edit the shape of curves and to change the direction of curves. You'll edit paths using the direction lines and direction points in a few minutes.

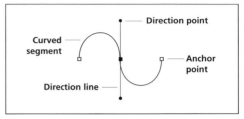

Direction lines and points setting the curve direction

Direction lines and points do not print when you print your artwork.

1 Choose File > Open. Locate and open the Lesson09 folder, then select Curves.psd and click Open.

2 Select the pen tool from the hidden tools palette in the toolbox.

3 Position the mouse button on point A of the first curve. *Hold down* the mouse button and drag toward the red dot.

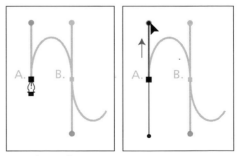

Dragging to draw a curve

4 To complete the first curve of the path, drag from point B to the red dot. If you make a mistake while you're drawing, choose Edit > Undo to undo the last point you drew; then continue drawing the path.

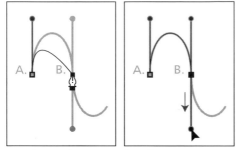

Continue to drag to complete the curve.

5 Complete the curved path by dragging from point C to the red dot and from point D to the red dot. End the path using one of the methods you learned.

6 Double-click the Work Path in the Paths palette to open the Save Path dialog box. Type the name **Curve1** and click OK to rename the path. The named path is selected in the Paths palette.

Sometimes, you'll want to create separate named paths for each path you draw. To start a new Work Path, you click away from the current path in the Paths palette.

7 In the Paths palette, click in the blank area below the Curve1 path to deselect the path.

When you deselect a path in the Paths palette, any paths on the named path are deselected (hidden). To make them reappear,

you click the desired path in the Paths palette (don't click the path now, because you're going to create a new one in a moment).

8 Drag up from point E to the red dot; then drag up from point F to the red dot. You'll notice that as soon as you begin drawing, a new Work Path appears in the Paths palette.

9 End the path using one of the methods you learned.

10 Double-click the Work Path in the Paths palette, name the path Curve2, and then click OK.

11 Click away from the path in the Paths palette to deselect it.

Now you'll create a closed curved path.

12 Drag up from point G to the red dot; then drag down from point H to the red dot. To close the path, position the pointer over point G and click.

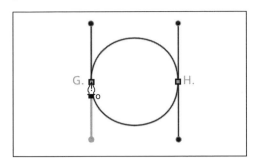

13 In the Paths palette, double-click the Work Path, save the path as Closed Path, and then click away from the path to deselect it.

Now you'll have a chance to edit the curved paths you've drawn.

14 Select the arrow tool (↖) from the hidden tools under the pen tool.

💡 Hold down Command (Macintosh) or Ctrl (Windows) when the pen tool is active to select the arrow tool from the keyboard.

15 In the Paths palette, click the Curve2 path to select it; then click the path in the window to select it.

16 Click one of the anchor points in the curve; then drag a direction point at the end the direction line emanating from the anchor point.

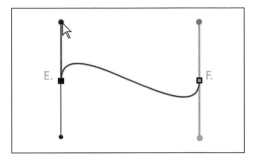

Dragging a direction point…

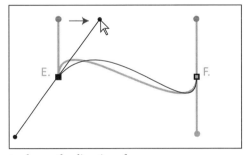

to change the direction of a curve.

17 Now, drag an anchor point to change the location of the curve.

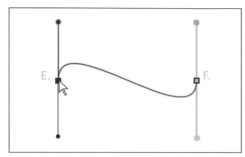

Dragging an anchor point…

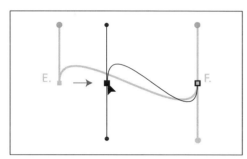

to change the location of the curve.

In addition to using the Stroke Subpath command, you can stroke paths by dragging a named path onto the Stroke Path button at the bottom of the Paths palette. To determine which painting option you want to stroke the path with, select the desired painting tool in the toolbox before you drag the path onto the Stroke Path button.

18 Click the paintbrush tool (✏) in the toolbox.

19 Drag the Curve1 path onto the Stroke Path button at the bottom of the Paths palette to stroke it with the current paintbrush settings.

Note: *You can also fill or stroke a path by clicking the Fill Path or Stroke Path button at the bottom of the Paths palette. Make sure that the path is selected in the palette before you click the button.*

20 Drag the Closed path onto the Fill Path button at the bottom of the Paths palette to fill it with the current foreground color.

(When you fill an open path, Photoshop automatically draws an invisible line between the starting point and the ending point, and fills the segments between them.)

21 Choose File > Close, and do not save changes.

Combining straight and curved lines

Now that you've learned how to draw straight and curved paths individually, you'll put them together to create paths that combine straight and curved lines.

To create a path that combines straight and curved lines, you create a *corner point* to indicate the transition from a straight line to a curved line (or vice versa).

1 Choose File > Open. Locate and open the Lesson09 folder, then select Combo.psd and click Open.

2 Select the pen tool in the toolbox.

3 Drag up from point A to the red dot; then drag from point B downward to the red dot.

4 At point B, you must create a corner point to change the direction of the next curve. Option-click (Macintosh) or Alt-click (Windows) point B; a corner point is set.

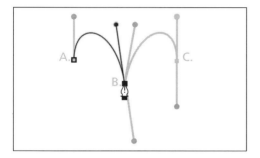

5 Now, drag from the same point (point B) up to the red dot to change the direction of the next curve.

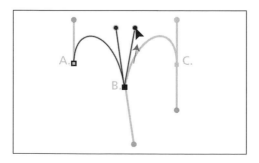

6 Drag from point C to the red dot to complete the path; then end the path using one of the methods you learned.

7 To start the second path, which begins with a straight line, click point D with the pen tool; then hold down Shift and click point E (don't drag).

8 Position the pen tool on point E and drag to the red dot. Dragging from point E sets the direction of the next curve (which is an upward curve).

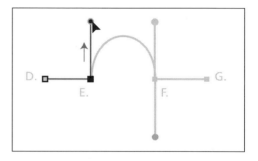

9 Drag from point F to the red dot; then Option-click (Macintosh) or Alt-click (Windows) point F to set a corner point.

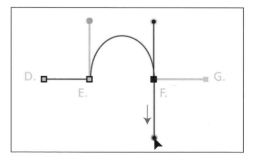

10 Hold down Shift and click point G to create a straight line, and then end the path using one of the methods you learned.

11 To create the next path, click the pen tool on point H, hold down Shift, and then click point I.

12 To set a curve at point I, Option-drag (Macintosh) or Alt-drag (Windows) the red dot.

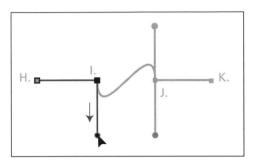

13 Drag from point J to the red dot.

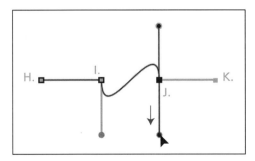

14 Option-click (Macintosh) or Alt-click (Windows) point J to set a corner point.

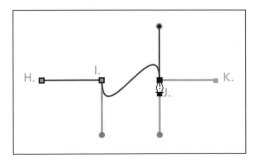

15 To complete the path, hold down Shift and click point K. End the path using one of the methods you learned.

16 Choose File > Close, and do not save changes.

Adding and subtracting anchor points

You can add points to a path to increase the number of segments in the path, and you can subtract unneeded or unwanted points from a path.

1 Choose File > Open. Locate and open the Lesson09 folder, then select Edit.psd and click Open.

Three paths have been created and saved in the Paths palette. You'll edit the paths using the pen tool and the convert-direction point tool.

2 Click the Paths palette tab to bring it to the front; then click the Add and Delete Points path to make it the active path. Two sub-paths appear in the window.

3 Select the add-anchor-point tool (✑₊) from the hidden tools palette in the toolbox; then position the tool over the red dot at the center of the straight path and click. An anchor point with direction lines is added to the segment.

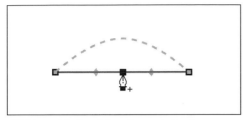

Clicking with the add-anchor-point tool

4 When you release the mouse button, the pointer becomes a hollow arrow, which lets you select and manipulate the path.

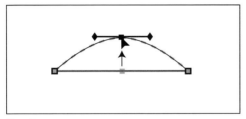

Result

Next, you'll subtract an anchor point from a path.

You can always select the arrow tool from the keyboard when the pen tool is active by holding down Command (Macintosh) or Ctrl (Windows).

5 Select the second path with the arrow tool. You must select the path before you can delete points from the path.

6 Select the delete-anchor-point tool (✒-) from the hidden tools palette, position it on the red dot over the center anchor point, and then click to remove the anchor point.

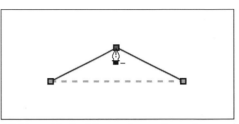

Clicking with the delete-anchor-point tool

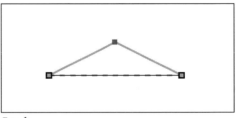

Result

Converting points

Sometimes, you may want to change a curve to a corner point or vice versa. Using the convert-direction-point tool, you can easily make the adjustment.

Using the convert-direction-point tool is very much like drawing with the pen tool. To convert a curve to a corner point, you click the anchor point, and to convert a corner to a curve, you drag on the anchor point.

1 In the Paths palette, click the path name Convert Directions to select it.

The shaped path has both corner points and curves. You'll start by converting the corner points to curves, and then you'll convert the curves to corner points.

2 Select the convert-direction-point tool (⌐) from the hidden tools palette.

3 Position the convert-direction-point tool on a point of the outer path; then drag to convert the point from a corner point to a curve.

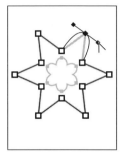

4 Convert the rest of the corner points to smooth points to complete the outer path.

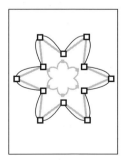

5 Now, to convert the curves at the center of the shape to corner points, simply click the anchor point on each curve.

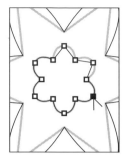

You can also use the convert-direction-point tool to adjust only one side of a curved segment. You'll try this on the outer path.

6 Click the outer path with the arrow tool; then click a curved segment so that direction lines and direction points emanate from one of the anchor points.

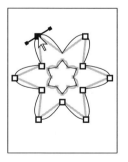

7 With the path still selected, position the convert-direction-point tool directly on one of the direction points (at the end of a direction line), and drag. Only one side of the curve is adjusted.

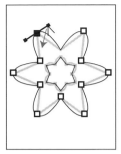 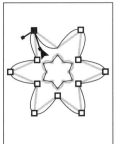

Dragging convert-direction-point tool   *Result*

Remember, you can use the convert-direction point tool to convert a corner point to a curve, to convert curve to a corner point, and to adjust one side of a curved segment.

8 Choose File > Close, and do not save changes.

Drawing a path around artwork

Now that you've had some practice using the templates, you'll draw a path around artwork in an image. After you've drawn the path, you'll convert it to a selection and then apply a filter to the selection to complete the image.

When drawing a freehand path using the pen tool, use as few points as possible to create the shape you want. The fewer points you use, the smoother the curves.

 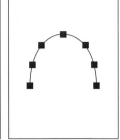

Correct number of points   *Too many points*

1 Choose File > Open. Locate and open the Lesson09 folder; then select Catmask.psd and click Open.

2 Choose File > Save As, enter the name **Catwork.psd**, and then click Save.

First you'll use the pen tool to draw a path around the outside of the mask. Then you'll create a path by creating a selection and then converting it to a path.

3 Select the pen tool from the hidden tools palette in the toolbox.

Press *p* on the keyboard to select the pen tool.

4 Position the pen tool on point A and drag to the red dot to set the first anchor point and the direction of the first curve.

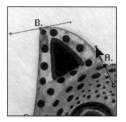

5 Position the pen tool on point B and drag to the red dot.

6 At the tip of the ear, you'll need to set a corner point. Option-click (Macintosh) or Alt-click (Windows) point B to set a corner point.

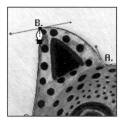

7 Now that you've set a corner point, position the pen tool on point C and drag to the red dot.

If you make a mistake while you're drawing, choose Edit > Undo to undo the step, then resume drawing.

The next few points are simple curves.

8 Position the pen tool on point D and drag to the red dot; then do the same for points E and F.

At point G, you'll complete the curve from point F and then you will need to set another corner point at the tip of the ear.

9 Position the pen tool on point G and drag to the red dot; then Option-click (Macintosh) or Alt-click (Windows) point G again to set a corner point.

10 Drag point H to the red dot (below the anchor point) to complete the curve of the ear.

11 Still on point H, Option-drag (Macintosh) or Alt-drag (Windows) to the yellow dot to set the direction of the final curve.

12 To end the path, Option-drag (Macintosh) or Alt-drag (Windows) point A to the yellow dot (which adds a slight curve to the line between the ears).

13 In the Paths palette, double-click the Work Path, name the path Face, and click OK to save it.

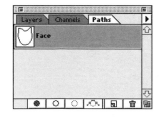

14 Choose File > Save to save your work.

Now you'll create a second path using a different method. First, you'll use a selection tool to select a similarly colored area, and then you'll convert the selection to a path.

15 Click the Layers palette tab to display the palette, and then drag the Template layer to the Trash button at the bottom of the palette. You won't need this layer any longer. Only the background should remain.

16 Double-click the magic wand tool (✎) in the toolbox. In the Magic Wand Options palette, enter 60 in the Tolerance text box.

17 Click the gray background where it shows through the cat's mouth.

18 If you don't select the entire area the first time, Shift-click again on the mouth with the magic wand to add to the selection.

19 Click the Paths palette tab to bring the Path palette to the front; then click the Make Path button at the bottom of the palette. The selection is converted to a path and a new Work Path is created.

Make Path

Note: If desired, use the tools you've learned to adjust the points on the path.

20 Double-click the Work Path and name it Mouth; then click OK to save the path.

21 Choose File > Save to save your work.

Converting paths to selections

You can convert paths to selections, and you can convert selection borders to paths. Now that you've drawn paths for the cat's face and mouth, you'll convert them to selections and apply a filter to the selection.

1 In the Paths palette, click the Face path to make it active.

2 Convert the Face path to a selection using either of the following methods:

• Choose Make Selection from the Paths palette menu.

• Drag the Face path to the Make Selection button at the bottom of the Paths palette.

Next, you'll subtract the mouth selection from the face selection so that you can apply a filter without affecting the gray area of the background, which shows through the cat's mouth.

3 In the Paths palette, click the Mouth path; then choose Make Selection from the Paths palette menu.

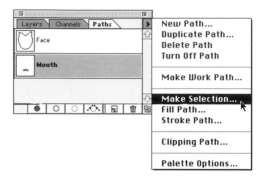

4 In the Make Selection dialog box, select Subtract from Selection in the Operation section; then click OK.

The Mouth path is simultaneously converted to a selection and subtracted from the Face selection.

5 Before adding a filter to the mask, make sure that the foreground is set to white and the background is set to black (if necessary, click the Switch Colors icon in the toolbox).

6 Choose Filter > Artistic > Neon Glow. Accept the defaults and click OK to apply the filter.

The filter has been applied to only the mask area. As a final step, you'll apply a textured filter to the entire image.

7 Choose Select > None to deselect everything.

8 Choose Filter > Texture > Texturizer. Select the Sandstone option from the Texture menu; then click OK to apply the settings.

9 Choose File > Save to save your work; then close the file.

You've completed the Basic Pen Tool lesson. Try drawing paths around different objects in your artwork to practice using the pen tool. With practice, you'll find that the pen tool can be invaluable for creating intricate outlines.

Review

• How do you draw straight paths with the pen tool?

• How do you draw curved paths with the pen tool?

• When you drag the pen tool to create a curved path, how does the direction in which you drag affect the curve?

• How do you draw paths that combine both straight and curved lines?

• How can the pen tool be useful as a selection tool?

10

Lesson 10

Basic Image Correction

The Adobe Photoshop tonal adjustment and color correction tools let you make adjustments to grayscale or color images and compensate for some of the differences between the original scanned image, the on-screen image, and the printed image. However, for your adjustments to be accurate for printing, your system must be calibrated. If you haven't yet calibrated your system, see Lesson 3, "Calibrating Your Monitor."

Restoring default preferences

Before starting this lesson, delete the Adobe Photoshop Preferences file to restore the program's default palettes and command settings. For step-by-step instructions about how to delete the preferences file, see "Restoring default preferences" on page 4.

Color management

It may seem as though matching the color of your on-screen images to the printed image should be a simple task, but because of the way scanners scan color, monitors display color, and inks print color, precise color-matching can be elusive, even to the best artist.

In addition, the perception of color can differ based on individual and environmental factors. If you've ever known someone who was color blind, you're probably already familiar with how the perception of color can vary; or if you've noticed how lighting changes in a room seem to alter the colors on your monitor, you have experienced how environmental influences can affect color.

Color adjustment in Adobe Photoshop and other digital art programs can be challenging to almost anyone in the desktop publishing industry. This lesson shows you how to use the Adobe Photoshop color-correction tools and commands to get the best possible results in your color images.

There are actually two parts to color management. First, you adjust the overall contrast, or *tonal range*, of an image, and then you make adjustments to the color values, if necessary.

Determining the tonal range of an image

The *tonal range* of an image (also known as the *dynamic range*) is determined by the way its pixels are distributed throughout the image's highlights, midtones, and shadows (from the darkest pixel to the lightest pixel in the image). See illustration 10–1 in the color section of this book for a sample of two image, one with sufficient tonal range, and one with insufficient tonal range.

Adobe Photoshop graphically displays the pixel distribution in an image using a *histogram*. The histogram displays the pixel values, based on their level of brightness, ranging from 0 (black) to 255 (white). The pixel values are plotted along the horizontal axis; the height of the graph at any point represents the total number of pixels in the image with that level of brightness. As you work with the color-correction tools, you can use the image's histogram to check for optimum brightness and contrast levels.

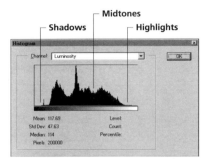

Histogram displaying pixel values and distribution

Determining the image type

Before you begin using the color-correction tools, it's a good idea to identify the type of image you're working with.

Images can be classified into one of three *key types*. The key type of an image is determined by the visual distribution of the tones within the image. When an image is composed of mostly dark tones, it is called a *low-key image*; when it is composed of mostly light tones, it is called a *high-key image*; and when the light and dark tones are about equal, it is called an *average-key image*.

You'll open three images, each of which is one of the key types. You'll be able to identify the key type of the image by the way the histogram displays the distribution of the pixels in the image.

1 Choose File > Open. Locate and open the Lesson10 folder; then select the Avgkey.psd file, and click Open.

2 Choose Image > Histogram. Click OK.

The Histogram dialog box displays the tonal range of the image (above the black-to-white bar) and shows statistical information about the pixels in the image at the bottom of the dialog box.

This image has an equal balance of light and dark tones, which identifies it as an average-key image. For a color sample of an average-key image, see illustration 10–2 in the color section of this book.

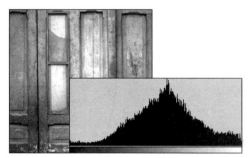

Pixel distribution in average-key image

3 Choose File > Open. Locate and open the Lesson10 folder; then select the Lowkey.psd file, and click Open.

4 Choose Image > Histogram. Click OK.

This image is composed of predominantly dark tones, so it is a low-key image. For a color sample of a low-key image, see illustration 10–3 in the color section of this book.

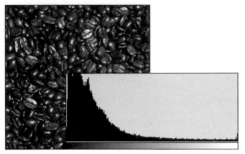

Pixel distribution in low-key image

5 Choose File > Open. Locate and open the Lesson10 folder; then select the Highkey.psd file, and click Open.

6 Choose Image > Histogram. Click OK.

This image is composed of predominantly light tones, so it is a high-key image. For a color sample of a high-key image, see illustration 10–4 in the color section of this book.

Pixel distribution in high-key image

7 Once you're taken a few minutes to look at the differences in the key types, close all the images, and do not save changes.

Working with the adjustment tools

The most commonly used adjustment tools are Brightness/Contrast, Levels, and Curves. The Brightness/Contrast command provides the simplest but most limited adjustment controls. The Levels command has more sophisticated adjustment controls, while the Curves command has the most sophisticated controls of all. In addition, the Auto Levels command is useful for automatically adjusting the tonal range of an image. You'll learn more about each command as you work through the sections that follow.

Using Brightness/Contrast to adjust an image

The Brightness/Contrast command offers the least amount of control over the tonal range of an image because the adjustment affects the image globally. For example, if you increase the brightness value by 20, all pixels in the image increase in brightness by a value of 20. See illustration 10–5 in the color section of this book for a sample.

The Brightness/Contrast command does not let you adjust individual channels within a document.

Dragging the Brightness slider lightens or darkens an image; dragging the Contrast slider increases or decreases the contrast in the image.

1 Choose File > Open. Locate and open the Lesson10 folder; then select the Bright.psd file, and click Open.

2 Choose Image > Adjust > Brightness/Contrast.

3 Drag the Brightness slider to 27, and drag the Contrast slider to 14. Click OK to adjust the brightness and contrast of the image.

4 Click OK to exit the dialog box; then close the file. Do not save changes.

Using auto levels

The Auto Levels command adjusts the overall contrast of an image by defining the lightest and darkest (highlight and shadow) pixels in an image as white and black, and then distributes the remaining tones in the image between them. The result that Auto Levels produces is determined by the characteristics of the original image. See illustration 10–6 in the color section of this book for a sample.

You'll apply the Auto Levels command to an image to see how the quality of the original scan affects the result.

1 Choose File > Open, locate the Lesson10 folder, select the Blossom.psd file, and click Open.

2 Choose Image > Adjust > Auto Levels. The image looks great!

3 Choose File > Close. Do not save changes.

Note: If the Auto Levels command produces an undesirable result, use the Levels dialog box to obtain greater control of the tonal range in the image. For information about how to use levels, see the following section, "Using levels."

Using levels

While the Auto Levels command controls the tonal balance of an image by automatically setting the lightest and darkest points in the image, the Levels command lets you control the tonal balance of an image by setting the lightest and darkest points in the image yourself. You can use Levels to affect an entire image, a selection, or a specific channel within an image. See illustration 10–7 in the color section of this book for a sample.

In addition, the Levels command lets you adjust the *gamma* in an image. Gamma measures the contrast that affects the mid-level grays (midtones), and can be adjusted without significantly affecting the shadows and highlights in an image.

You'll work with the controls in the Levels dialog box to adjust the highlights and shadows of an image using two methods. First, you'll drag the sliders in the dialog box to adjust the highlights and shadows, and then you'll define and set the highlights and shadows by choosing values from the image.

Adjusting the tonal range of an initial scan using Levels sliders

Most initial scans require an adjustment to the tonal balance of the image before making other color adjustments. You'll use the Levels dialog box first to adjust the tonal range of a scanned image.

1 Choose File > Open. Locate and open the Lesson10 folder, select the Fruit.psd file, and click Open.

2 Choose Image > Adjust > Levels.

The Levels dialog box displays a histogram of the image and a variety of controls that let you adjust the tonal range of the image. At this point, focus on the three triangles at the bottom of the histogram. The white triangle represents the highlight areas of the image, the gray triangle represents the midtones in the image, and the black triangle represents the shadow areas of the image.

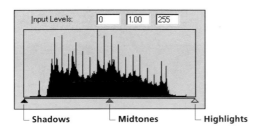

Notice that the black triangle (at the left end of the histogram) is positioned to the left of the point at which the pixels in the image actually start. The same is true of the white triangle at the right end of the histogram; it is positioned to the right of the point where the pixels in the image actually end.

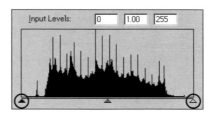

When the black and white triangles are positioned outside the actual starting and ending pixels in the image, the image looks "flat," because there is a lack of contrast in both the highlights and shadows of the image. As a general rule, most initial scans come in flat and need an initial adjustment to redefine the black point, the gamma, and the white point.

3 Drag the black slider to the right to position it under the starting pixels in the histogram; then drag the white slider to the left to position it under the ending pixels in the image.

4 Drag the gamma slider to the right to lighten the midtones of the image a bit. The value should be about 80, but each monitor looks slightly different, so the level of adjustment may vary slightly.

5 Click OK. The pixels are redistributed from black to white, extending the tonal range of the image.

6 Choose Edit > Undo several times to see the difference before and after the adjustment.

7 Choose Image > Adjust > Levels. Now the histogram reflects the redistribution of the pixels from black to white.

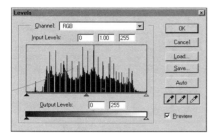

8 Choose File > Close. Do not save changes.

It's a good practice to follow this procedure for all initial scans.

Assigning values to the black and white points

Now that you've learned one method to adjust the tonal range of an initial scan, you'll use some of the other controls in the Levels dialog box to define and set your own shadows and highlights (called black and white points) in an image. See illustration 10–8 in the color section of this book for a sample.

This time, instead of using the sliders to adjust the contrast of the image (by moving the triangles), you'll enter values to define the darkest and lightest points in the image.

When you define the values of the black and white points, you ensure that both areas hold detail when printed. If the highlight area of an image contains no detail, no ink is printed on the paper; this white without detail is called *specular white*. If the shadow area of an image contains no detail, the paper is saturated with black ink, producing a solid-black area.

1 Choose File > Open. Locate and open the Lesson10 folder; then select the Market.psd file, and click Open.

2 Choose Image > Adjust > Levels; then double-click the white eyedropper tool to open the Color Picker, where you enter values to define the white point.

In a typical printing situation, where you are printing an average-key image on white paper, the CMYK values for the white point (highlight areas) should be about 5, 3, 3, 0. (The RGB values would be 244, 244, 244.)

3 Enter 5, 3, 3, and 0 in the CMYK text boxes in the Color Picker. Click OK.

4 Now double-click the black eyedropper tool in the Levels dialog box to open the Color Picker and set the value for the black point.

Again, in a typical printing situation, where you are printing an average-key image on white paper, the CMYK values for the black point (shadow areas) should be about 65, 53, 51, and 95. (The RGB values would be 10, 10, and 10.)

5 Enter **65**, **53**, **51**, and **95** in the CMYK text boxes and click OK.

Now that you have defined the values for the black and white points, you'll use the eyedropper to select and define the black and white areas in the image.

6 With the black eyedropper tool in the Levels dialog box still selected, position the pointer in the dark area of the lower left corner of the image. Click the eyedropper tool to define this area as the darkest point in the image.

7 Click the white eyedropper tool, and then position it in the price slip labeled $1.99 near the center of the image. Click the white area to define the lightest point in the image.

8 Adjust midtones by dragging the middle (gamma) Levels slider.

9 Click OK to close the dialog box.

10 Choose Edit > Undo several times to see the difference before and after the adjustment.

11 Choose File > Close. Do not save changes.

Using curves

The Curves dialog box provides the most sophisticated controls of the tonal adjustment tools. In addition to using Curves to set the black and white points, you can control the midtones in an image with greater precision. See illustration 10–9 in the color section of this book for a sample.

You'll use the Curves dialog box to adjust the midtones in an image. (The highlights and shadows have already been set.)

1 Choose File > Open, locate the Lesson10 folder, select the Floral.psd file, and click Open.

2 Choose Image > Adjust > Curves.

The Curves dialog box displays a graph that represents the original and new brightness values of the pixels in the image. The horizontal axis represents the original values of the pixels, and the vertical axis represents the new (adjusted) values of the pixels. At this point, the original pixel values, called *input values*, and the new pixels values, called *output values*, are the same, because you haven't made an adjustment to the image.

The diagonal line in the graph represents the current relationship between the input values and output values. The bottom left corner point of the diagonal line represents the shadows in the image; the midpoint in the line represents the midtones in the image, and the top right corner point represents the highlights in the image.

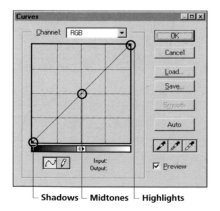

Shadows — **Midtones** — **Highlights**

Below the graph, a black-to-white bar displays the pixel brightness values from black to white (0 to 255, respectively).

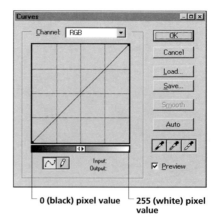

0 (black) pixel value — **255 (white) pixel value**

To get an idea of how the Curves graph identifies pixel brightness values in an image, move the pointer into the Floral image window (it becomes an eyedropper), and slowly drag the eyedropper on different areas of the image.

As you drag, you'll notice a moving circle on the diagonal line on the graph. When you drag the eyedropper in a dark area of the image, the circle is near the lower left of the diagonal line; when you drag in a light area of the image, the circle moves toward the top of the diagonal line, representing the highlights and shadows.

Dragging the eyedropper in the image window to display the pixel values in the Curves dialog box

This image requires an adjustment to the midtone and shadow areas, but not to the highlights. To make the adjustment to only the midtones and shadows, you can set points along the diagonal line to isolate the areas you don't want affected. You'll set two points along the diagonal line.

3 Click the pointer on the quarter-tone point along the diagonal line (the curve).

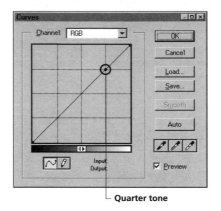

Quarter tone

4 Click the pointer on the three-quarter-tone point along the diagonal line (the curve)

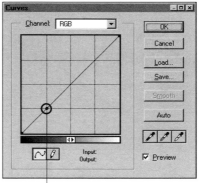

Three-quarter tone

5 Now drag the three-quarter-tone point upward to lighten the shadows and midtones in the image. By anchoring the curve at the three-quarter-tone point, none of the highlights in the image is affected.

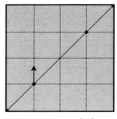 

Using curves to lighten shadows and midtones   *Result*

6 Click OK to make the adjustment to the floral image.

7 Choose File > Close. Do not save changes.

Removing a color cast

Now that you've worked with the tonal correction tools, you'll use a color correction command to remove a color cast from an image. The Color Balance command lets you change the mixture of colors in a color image. Like the Brightness/Contrast command, this tool provides generalized color correction. See illustration 10–9 in the color section of this book for a sample.

1 Choose File > Open. Locate and open the Lesson10 folder; then select Brdhouse.psd and click Open.

2 Choose Image > Adjust > Color Balance to open the Color Balance dialog box.

3 Before you begin making adjustments, make sure the Preview option is selected in the dialog box.

4 Drag the first slider to –22 (toward cyan); then drag the second slider to 29 (toward green). These settings remove the magenta cast from the image.

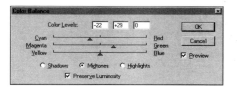

You've completed the Basic Color Correction lesson. The project that follows, "Photo Retouching," shows additional color-correction tools you can use once you've learned the basic techniques.

5 Click OK; then choose File > Close to close the file. Do not save changes.

Look over the questions and answers in the Review section to help you identify and retain key concepts about color correction.

Review

• What is tonal range? Tonal balance?

• How does a histogram depict the tonal range of an image?

• What are the different tonal correction tools, and why would you use one over another?

• What is a color cast?

C

Project C
Photo Retouching

Once you've scanned an image and opened it in Adobe Photoshop, there are several basic retouching steps you should follow to maximize the quality of the final image. If you are using your monitor to measure the adjustments you make, be sure to calibrate your monitor before you begin the adjustment process. For more information, see Lesson 3, "Calibrating Your Monitor."

This project teaches you some new photo retouching techniques and reviews some techniques that were introduced in the previous lesson. This project shows you how to do the following:

• Realign part of an image using guides.

• Crop an image to a final size.

• Adjust the tonal range of a scanned image.

• Remove a color cast from an image using an adjustment layer.

• Adjust the tonal range of a selected area of an image using the Levels command.

• Use the Replace Color command to change the color of one of the elements in a photograph.

• Use the Navigator palette to move around an image.

• Adjust the hue and saturation of part of an image.

• Use the rubber stamp tool to eliminate an unwanted object from an image.

• Apply the Unsharp Mask filter to finalize the photo-retouching process.

Restoring default preferences

Before starting this lesson, delete the Adobe Photoshop Preferences file to restore the program's default palettes and command settings. For step-by-step instructions about how to delete the preferences file, see "Restoring default preferences" on page 4. After you've deleted the preferences file, restart Adobe Photoshop.

Getting started

Before you begin working, you'll open the final image to see how the adjustments you'll make will affect the final artwork.

1 Choose File > Open. Locate and open the ProjectC folder; then select EndC.psd and click Open.

2 If desired, choose View > Zoom Out to make the image smaller, and leave it on your screen as you work. If you don't want to leave the image open, choose File > Close.

Now you'll open the initial scan of the photograph of a building.

3 Choose File > Open. Locate and open the ProjectC folder; then select StartC.psd and click Open.

4 Choose File > Save As, enter the name WorkC.psd, and click Save.

Basic retouching steps

Although some of the retouching techniques you'll use to correct the building image are optional, be sure to apply the following basic retouching steps to all images after an initial scan:

• Crop the image to a final size.

• Adjust the tonal range of the image using the Levels and Curves commands.

- Remove any color casts (if they exist).

- Adjust the tonal range in specific parts of the image to bring out highlights, midtones, or shadows (as needed).

- Apply the Unsharp Mask filter.

Realigning an image using guides

You use guides to align artwork in an image. For the building photograph, you'll set guides at the sides of the building, and then use the Free Transform command to straighten the angles at the sides of the building. (The original photograph was shot at an angle, causing a distorted perspective.)

1 Choose View > Show Rulers to display the rulers in the document window.

To create a guide, you drag from either the horizontal or vertical ruler.

2 Drag a guide from the vertical ruler to the left side of the building. Make sure that the guide is positioned inside the boundary of the upper left side of the building.

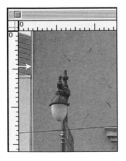

3 Drag a guide from the vertical ruler to the right side of the building. Make sure that the guide is positioned inside the boundary of the upper right side of the building.

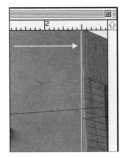

4 If you need to reposition either of the guides, select the move tool in the toolbox, position it on the guide, and then drag to move the guide.

Next, you'll make a selection that extends outside the boundary of the guides, to adjust the perspective of the entire front of the building. The selection marquee must encompass the entire face of the building. To make the marquee encompass the entire face of the building, you will start and end outside the boundary of the guides.

5 Select the rectangle marquee tool in the toolbox.

6 Before making the selection, visually identify the lower left corner and the lower right corner of the face of the building. The selection marquee must include both of these corners.

7 Position the pointer at the lower left corner of the building, and drag diagonally upward. As you drag upward, keep an eye on the lower right corner of the selection marquee (but don't release the mouse button). When the bottom right corner of the selection marque touches the lower right corner of the face of the building, release the mouse button.

8 Choose Layer > Free Transform. The bounding border appears around the selection marquee.

9 Choose File > Save to save your work.

To straighten the sides of the building, you must move each segment of the bounding border inward.

10 Hold down Command (Macintosh) or Ctrl (Windows), and drag the lower left anchor point of the bounding border in toward the guide (to the right). (The pointer turns into a black arrowhead inside the border.)

Note: Holding down Command/Ctrl lets you move individual segments of the bounding border.

11 When the corner point is aligned with the guide, release the mouse button. The left segment of the bounding border moves and the side of the building is realigned.

12 Hold down Command (Macintosh) or Ctrl (Windows), and drag the lower right anchor point of the bounding border in toward the guide (to the left).

13 When the corner point is aligned with the guide, release the mouse button. The right segment of the bounding border moves and the side is realigned.

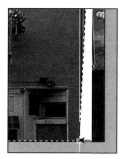

14 Press Return (Macintosh) or Enter (Windows) to apply the transformation.

15 Choose View > Hide Guides to turn off the display of the guides.

16 Choose Select > None to deselect everything.

17 Select the crop tool (⛏) from the hidden tools under the rectangle marquee.

Press *c* on the keyboard to select the crop tool in the toolbox.

18 Drag a crop marquee to select the front of the building. If you need to adjust the marquee, drag the handles surrounding the crop marquee.

19 Press Return (Macintosh) or Enter (Windows) to crop the image.

20 Choose File > Save to save your work.

Adjusting the tonal range

As you learned in the previous lesson, the tonal range of an image represents the amount of *contrast*, or detail, in an image,

and is determined by the distribution of the pixels in the image, ranging from the darkest pixels (black) to the lightest pixels (white).

You will adjust the tonal range of the building image, but this time you'll use an Adjustment Layer in conjunction with the Levels command. Adjustment layers let you make a temporary adjustment to the pixels in the image without causing a permanent change. You can edit the levels of the image as many times as you like without ever changing the original pixel values.

1 Choose Layer > New > Adjustment Layer. In the New Adjustment Layer dialog box, make sure that Levels is selected for Type.

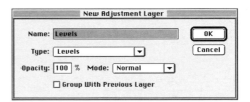

2 Click OK to create the adjustment layer and to display the Levels dialog box.

3 Make sure that Preview is selected in the Levels dialog box.

In the previous lesson, you learned that the three triangles at the bottom of the histogram represent the shadows, midtones (gamma), and highlight areas of the image. You'll adjust the black and white points of the original scanned image to extend its tonal range.

4 At the left side of the histogram, drag the black triangle in to the right to position it where the pixels (represented by black) begin.

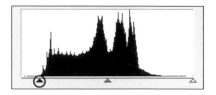

5 At the right side of the histogram, drag the white triangle in to the left to position it where the black pixels (represented by black) begin.

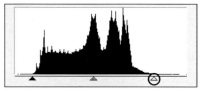

Setting new black and white points

6 Click OK to apply the changes.

7 Choose File > Save to save your work.

Removing a color cast

Some images contain color casts (imbalances of color), which may occur during scanning or which may have existed in the original image.

Note: To see a color cast in an image on your monitor, you need a 24-bit monitor (one that can display millions of colors). On monitors that can display only 256 colors (8-bits), a color cast is difficult, if not impossible to detect.

You can also use adjustment layers to remove color casts. If you plan to print your images or generate color proofs, you should use an adjustment layer to correct a color cast. By using an adjustment layer, you can make additional changes, if necessary, after you see the color proof or the printed image.

1 Choose Layer > New > Adjustment Layer.

2 For Type, choose Color Balance; then click OK.

3 Drag the top triangle to the right to +15 (toward red), and drag the second triangle to the left to −29 (toward magenta).

4 Click OK to apply the changes to the Color Balance adjustment layer.

Notice the Color Balance layer in the Layers palette.

5 In the Layers palette, click the eye icon next to the Color Balance layer to hide and show the layer. You'll see the difference between the adjusted colors and the original colors.

6 Choose File > Save to save your work.

Note: When you double-click an adjustment layer in the Layers palette, the corresponding dialog box appears, where you can edit the values of the adjustment layer repeatedly.

Adjusting the tonal range of selected areas of an image

In addition to adjusting the tonal range of an entire image, you can adjust selected areas. You'll enhance the shadows in the area of the image near the awning and the lower windows.

1 Double-click the lasso tool in the toolbox. In the Lasso Options palette, enter a value of 10 for the Feather Radius.

2 Using the lasso tool, draw a loose selection around the lower windows, the awning, and the doorway.

3 Choose Layer > New > Adjustment Layer. For Type, choose Levels, and click OK to create the layer and to open the Levels dialog box.

4 Drag the white triangle in to the left to bring out the highlights in the selection; then click OK.

5 In the Layers palette, click the eye icon next to the Levels adjustment layer to view and hide the layer. You'll notice the difference in the tonal range of the shadow areas.

6 Choose File > Save to save your work.

Replacing colors in an image

The Replace Color command lets you select and replace colors in an image. You'll replace the color of the windows.

1 In the Layers palette, select the Background.

2 Select the rectangle marquee tool from the toolbox and drag a selection marquee around the windows. Don't worry about making a perfect selection, but do be sure to include all the window frames in the selection.

3 Choose Image > Adjust > Replace Color to open the Replace Color dialog box.

By default, the Selection area of the Replace Color dialog box displays a black rectangle, representing the current selection.

Three eyedropper tools are displayed in the Replace Color dialog box.

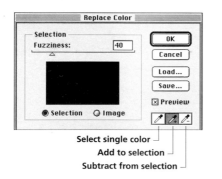

Select single color —
Add to selection —
Subtract from selection —

You use the eyedropper tools to select the colors you want to replace. The first eyedropper selects a single color, the eyedrop-

per-plus tool is used to add colors to a selection, and the eyedropper-minus tool is used to subtract colors from a selection.

4 Click the eyedropper-plus tool; then position it in the image window and drag through the turquoise colors in the window frame (don't drag through the window-panes).

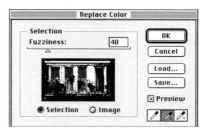

Now the area displays the selected parts of the image in white.

5 Drag the Hue slider to –38, and then drag the Saturation slider to –11. The colors in the window frames are replaced with the new hue and saturation.

6 Click OK to apply the changes.

7 Choose Select > None to deselect everything.

Adjusting hue and saturation

The Hue/Saturation command is used to adjust the hue, saturation, and brightness of individual color components in an image. *Hue* is color, *saturation* is the purity of the color, and *brightness* is how much white or black there is in the image.

You'll enhance the color in the flowers using the Hue/Saturation command.

1 Click the zoom tool in the toolbox, then click and drag a marquee around the flowers on the balcony.

2 Double-click the lasso tool in the toolbox.

3 In the Lasso Options palette, enter **0** for Feather.

4 Drag the lasso tool around the yellow flowers; then choose Image > Adjust > Hue/Saturation.

5 Drag the Hue slider to change the hue of the selected flowers to a color that appeals to you.

6 Drag the Saturation slider to the left to reduce the saturation of the new hue, if necessary.

If desired, drag the Lightness slider to vary the lightness or darkness of the flowers; then click OK.

7 Choose View > Hide Edges to preview the results without the selection marquee.

8 Choose View > Show Edges to view the selection marquee.

9 Choose Select > None to deselect everything.

Removing unwanted objects

One of the most fun (and amazing) aspects of photo retouching with Adobe Photoshop is the ability to remove unwanted objects from a photograph. Using the rubber stamp tool, you can remove an unwanted object or area by "cloning" an area of the image over the area you want to eliminate.

You'll remove the wire that runs across the front of the building—and you'll be amazed when you've finished, because no one will ever suspect it was there in the original photograph!

1 Double-click the hand tool to fit the image in the window.

2 Choose File > Preferences > Display & Cursors. For Painting Cursors, click Brush Size; then click OK.

3 Select the rubber stamp tool (⬚) in the toolbox.

Using the rubber stamp tool, you begin by defining an area of the image you will use to paint over the undesirable area. In this case, you'll use the face of the building as the cloning area.

4 Click the Brushes palette tab to bring the palette to the front. In the Brushes palette, select a small brush from the second row of brushes. The brush size you select is the size of the brush that will be used to paint out the wire.

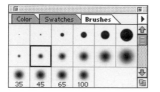

5 To select the cloning area, hold down Option (Macintosh) or Alt (Windows), and click the rubber stamp tool about half an inch above the wire anywhere on the face of the building.

Above the rubber stamp location, you'll notice a crosshair. The crosshair represents the point from which the rubber stamp tool duplicates, or clones, the area.

6 Position the rubber stamp tool on the wire and drag to replace the wire with the colors from the face of the building.

For best results, use short strokes when replacing areas of an image with the rubber stamp tool.

7 To vary the cloning area a bit, resample different areas of the face of the building by holding down the Option (Macintosh) or Alt (Windows) key and clicking the rubber stamp. Sampling different cloning areas makes the completed image look realistic.

The rubber stamp tool has several options that let you clone areas in different ways. For complete information about the rubber stamp options, see the *Adobe Photoshop User Guide*.

8 As a final touch, select the lasso tool, enter 4 for Feather in the Lasso Options palette, and then select the white lantern of the street lamp.

9 Choose a yellow color from the Swatches palette. Then choose Edit > Fill, enter 30% for Opacity, and select Color for mode.

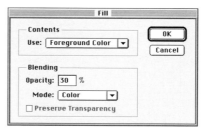

10 Click OK to apply the changes. The street lamp is turned on!

11 Choose Select > None to deselect every-thing.

12 Choose File > Save to save your work.

Applying the Unsharp Mask filter

The last step you take when retouching a photo is to apply the Unsharp Mask filter to the image. The Unsharp Mask filter adjusts the contrast of the edge detail in an image, creating the illusion of a sharper image.

1 Choose Filter > Sharpen > Unsharp Mask.

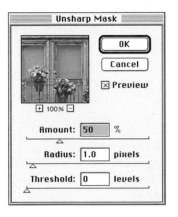

2 Drag the Amount slider to about 40%; then click OK to apply the Unsharp Mask filter.

Note: For high-resolution printed images, the Amount value is set to a higher value. For more information about the Unsharp Mask filter, see Chapter 6, "Making Color and Tonal Adjustments," in the Adobe Photoshop User Guide.

You've completed all of the steps necessary to retouch a photo. Try these steps and techniques on your own scanned images.

11

Lesson 11

Sharing Files Between Applications

Adobe Photoshop can open and save files in more than 20 file formats. To open an Adobe Photoshop file in another program, you save the file in a format the application can read. For example, to open a Photoshop file in Adobe Illustrator, you save the Photoshop file in Photoshop EPS format because Adobe Illustrator reads Photoshop EPS files.

In this lesson, you'll learn how to do the following:

• Place an Adobe Illustrator file in an Adobe Photoshop file.

• Understand the difference between the Save As and Save a Copy commands, and use the Save a Copy command to save files to other file formats.

• Understand how file data is compressed when you save files in certain formats, and determine the appropriate compression options for specific types of images.

• Save files in EPS, JPEG, PICT, and TIFF file formats.

• Create a clipping path in an EPS image for use in an Adobe Illustrator file.

• Save an Adobe Photoshop File with an alpha channel for use in video-editing software.

Restoring default preferences

Before starting this lesson, delete the Adobe Photoshop Preferences file to restore the program's default palettes and command settings. For step-by-step instructions about how to delete the preferences file, see "Restoring default preferences" on page 4. After you've deleted the preferences file, restart Adobe Photoshop.

Opening and placing Adobe Illustrator files

You can open an Adobe Illustrator file as an Adobe Photoshop file, or you can place an Adobe Illustrator file into an existing Adobe Photoshop file. When you choose the Open command in Adobe Photoshop, the Adobe Illustrator file is opened as a new Adobe Photoshop file. When you choose the Place command in Adobe Photoshop, the Adobe Illustrator file is placed in an existing open Adobe Photoshop file.

When you open or place an Adobe Illustrator image, Adobe Photoshop rasterizes the image. *Rasterizing* is the process of converting an Adobe Illustrator file, which is a vector image, into a pixel-based, or raster, image. For more information, see "Vector and raster images" in Lesson 2, Image Basics.

Why use an Adobe Illustrator file?

Adobe Illustrator lets you create type on a path of any shape. Although you can create, scale, and rotate type in Adobe Photoshop, you can't add type to shaped paths.

In addition, you can open an Adobe Illustrator file in Photoshop to apply transparency or to further manipulate the original image.

Placing type from an Adobe Illustrator file

Using the Place command, you will import an Adobe Illustrator file containing type on a shaped path into the image of the CDs.

1 Choose File > Open, locate and open the Lesson11 folder, then select the Start11.psd file and click Open.

2 Choose File > Place. In the Lesson11 folder, select Text.ai from the list of files and click Place (Macintosh) or Open (Windows).

The type appears within a rectangle in the Photoshop image, and a new layer is created for the type in the Layers palette.

3 To scale the type to fit on the CD, drag one of the handles at a corner of the rectangle. To scale the type proportionately, hold down Shift as you drag the handle.

4 Hold down Command (Macintosh) or Ctrl (Windows) to select the move tool (⊹) from the keyboard; then drag to reposition the type over the CD.

5 Press Return to place the type.

6 In the Layers palette, click the text layer to select it. Then drag the Opacity slider to 90% to make the text semitransparent.

7 Choose File > Save As, name the file Work11.psd, and click Save.

Saving Adobe Photoshop files

Once you have completed an Adobe Photoshop image, you may want to export it to a page-layout program or to a drawing program to add type or to combine the image with another type of file.

This lesson describes the file formats accepted by most programs—Photoshop EPS, JPEG, PICT, and TIFF. For information about all the available file formats, see Chapter 13, "Saving and Exporting Files," in the *Adobe Photoshop User Guide*.

Understanding compression

Before you save an Adobe Photoshop image in another file format, you'll learn about compression. The term *compression* refers to the way file data is conserved when a file is saved.

There are two basic types of compression: *lossy*, which discards information when the file is saved, and *lossless*, which does not discard information when the file is saved.

Saving files in other formats

Adobe Photoshop provides three ways to save a file—the Save, Save As, and Save a Copy commands. When you choose the Save or Save As commands to save a file in a format other than Adobe Photoshop, the file must be prepared to save in the new file format. For example, to save an Adobe Photoshop file containing multiple layers in Photoshop EPS format, you must prepare the file by flattening all of the layers in the file. On the Macintosh, if you don't flatten the file first, the EPS option is unavailable (dimmed) in the format menu. For Windows, if you don't flatten the file first, the Adobe Photoshop file format is the only one displayed.

The Save a Copy command is a one-step way to prepare a file for saving in any file format. For example, the Save a Copy command automatically selects the Flatten option for

an Adobe Photoshop file containing multiple layers when you select the Photoshop EPS file format.

File with layers saved in EPS using Save a Copy

In this lesson, use the Save a Copy command each time you save a file in a new format, instead of the Save As command.

Saving in EPS file format

The Encapsulated PostScript file (EPS) format is supported by most illustration and page-layout programs, and in most cases is the preferred format for these applications. If you plan to export an Adobe Photoshop file for use in Adobe Illustrator, make sure that the image is in CMYK mode before you save it as an EPS file (so that the file is separated by Adobe Photoshop).

1 Make sure that the Work11.psd image is active; then choose File > Save a Copy.

2 In the Save dialog box, for Format choose Photoshop EPS. Notice that when you choose Photoshop EPS as the file format, the Flatten Image option is dimmed at the bottom of the Save dialog box.

Hold down Option (Macintosh) or Alt (Windows) as you select a format from the format menu to automatically add the 3-character file extension to the filename.

3 Click Save. The EPS Format dialog box appears, from which you select options for the EPS image.

4 Choose one of the following options to indicate how you want a preview of the image to appear in the page-layout or drawing program:

• On either the Macintosh or in Windows, choose a TIFF option from the Preview menu to save a preview image for use with an IBM PC-compatible application. A 1-bit image preview appears in black and white; an 8-bit image appears in 256 colors. (On the Macintosh, you can save a 24-pit JPEG preview if you have QuickTime installed.)

• In Windows, choose None to not display a preview of the image in the page-layout or drawing program.

5 Choose one of the following Encoding options to determine what type of information is saved in a file:

• Select Binary to create a file that is about half the size of a file saved with the ASCII encoding option, and that takes half as long to transfer to the printer.

• Select ASCII for some of the commercial print spooling and network printing software that may not support binary EPS files.

• Select a JPEG compression option; for more information, see Chapter 13, "Saving and Exporting Files," in the *Adobe Photoshop User Guide.*

6 If you plan to use a path from an Adobe Photoshop file as a clipping path in a page-layout program, select the named path from the menu and set a flatness value, if necessary. See "Creating clipping paths" on page 222 for more information on clipping paths and clipping path options.

7 As an option, choose to include the EPS file halftone screen information (including the frequencies and angles of the screens) and transfer function information when you save the EPS file.

If you include the halftone screen information and place it into another application, such as Adobe Separator, halftone screen information overrides the settings in the application you place the file in (when color separations are generated). The transfer information overrides the printer's default functions if you have checked the Override Printer's Default Functions option in the Transfer Functions dialog box. For more information about transfer function and half-tone screens, see Chapter 5, "Reproducing Color" in the *Adobe Photoshop User Guide.*

8 As an option, if you're saving a CMYK file in EPS format, also save the file as a Desktop Color Separations (DCS) file.

DCS is an extension of the standard EPS format, developed by Quark, that lets certain applications, such as QuarkXPress, to read imported Photoshop files and print color separations. When you save a file using the DCS option, five files are created. Each of the four color channels (C, M, Y, and K) is saved as a single file, and a fifth file containing a low-resolution preview of the composite channel is also saved.

9 As an option if you saved a CMYK or grayscale image in the DCS format, also choose to include a low-resolution (72-ppi) color or grayscale version of the image in the master file. You can then proof the image by printing this low-resolution file from the destination application; keep in mind, however, that selecting one of these options may substantially increase the file size. If you're certain that you will print directly to film, choose the On (no composite PostScript) option.

10 Click OK to save the file; then choose File > Close to close the file.

Creating clipping paths

By default, when you export an Adobe Photoshop file to a page-layout program, the entire image is opaque, including the background. For example, if an object shot against a white background is placed in a page-layout program, the white background appears as an opaque background in the page-layout file.

Sometimes you'll want to export a Photoshop image and hide, or *clip,* the background so that only the desired portion of the image is visible. To isolate part of an image when it is exported, you create a *clipping path* in the Adobe Photoshop image before exporting it to the page-layout program. Everything outside the isolated area appears transparent when the image is printed or placed in another application.

Look at the following examples of the same image exported from Adobe Photoshop to Adobe Illustrator. The first example shows the file exported without a clipping path; the second example shows the same file exported with a clipping path. For a color sample of an image saved with a clipping path, see illustration 11–1 in the color section of this book.

Placed Photoshop file, exported without clipping path

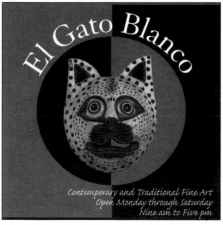

Placed Photoshop file, exported with clipping path

Now, you'll open an Adobe Photoshop image that already contains a path. You will define the path as a clipping path, and then export the image with the clipping path.

(The paths in the Photoshop image were created using the pen tool. For information about how to use the pen tool to draw paths, see Lesson 9, "Basic Pen Tool Techniques.")

1 Choose File > Open. Locate and open the Lesson11 folder; then select Clipping.psd and click Open.

2 Click the Paths palette tab, and then click the Cat Mask path to display the path in the image window.

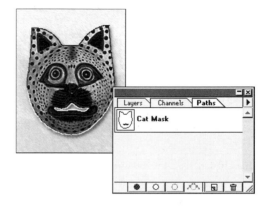

Note: Paths must be named before they can be used as clipping paths.

3 From the Paths palette menu, choose Clipping Path.

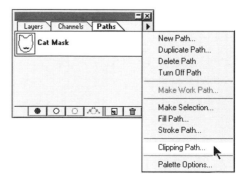

The Paths dialog box appears, where you choose the path you want to assign as a clipping path.

4 For Path, choose Cat Mask, and click OK.

The path name appears outlined (Macintosh) or in bold (Windows) in the Paths palette to indicate that it is a clipping path.

Next, you save the file in Photoshop EPS format.

5 Choose File > Save a Copy.

6 Now, hold down Option (Macintosh) or Alt (Windows) and choose Photoshop EPS from the Format menu. Using Option/Alt while selecting a file format automatically adds the correct 3-character extension to the file name (in this case it is .eps).

7 Click Save; the EPS Format dialog box appears.

8 Leave the remaining options unchanged, and click OK to save the file.

9 Open the page-layout program of your choice, and import the saved .eps file. (We imported the image into Adobe Illustrator.)

10 Choose File > Close. Do not save changes.

Note: *For Windows, the clipping path will not preview correctly, but it will print properly.*

Saving in the JPEG file format

Joint Photographic Experts Group (JPEG) compression economizes on the way data is stored, and identifies and discards extra data not essential to the display of the image. Because it discards data, the JPEG algorithm is referred to as *lossy*. Once an image has been compressed and then decompressed using lossy compression, it will not match the original image. In most cases, the difference between the original image and the image compressed using the Excellent JPEG option is indistinguishable. However, the type of image you compress also determines the difference in the image once it has been compressed and decompressed. Use the following guidelines to determine which JPEG option you should select:

• For images that contains soft edges and similar colors—for example, the fern image shown in illustration 11–2 in the color section of this book—you can use the Small File/Low Quality option without seeing much of a difference when the file is decompressed.

• For images that contain sharp contrast—for example, the reeds image, also shown in illustration 11–2—select a Large File/High or Maximum Quality option.

A trade-off exists between the image quality and the amount of compression. An image compressed using the Maximum setting is less compressed (and thus a larger file) than an image compressed using the Low setting. In general, images compressed using the Maximum setting have compression ratios between 5:1 and 15:1. JPEG images are automatically decompressed when opened.

You'll open two identical images saved with different compression options to see the difference in compression quality.

1 Choose File > Open. Locate and open the Lesson11 folder; then select the Low.jpg file, and click Open.

2 Choose File > Open; then select the Max.jpg file, and click Open.

3 Align the images side-by-side to examine the difference in the image quality.

The quality of the lettering is diminished in the image saved with the Low Quality setting, and appears pixelated. (For a printed sample, see 11–2 in the color section.)

Now, you'll select the two files in the Open dialog box to compare the file size. In general, the higher compression setting you select, the larger the file.

4 Choose File > Open again, select the Low.jpg image in the list of files and notice its size (about 64K).

5 Choose File > Open again, select the Max.jpg image in the list of files and notice its size (about 224K).

6 Close both images, and if prompted, do not save changes.

Important: Do not save JPEG files repeatedly, because each time you save the file, more data is removed, causing potential image degradation.

Saving PICT files (raster only)

The raster PICT format is widely used among Macintosh graphics and page-layout programs as an intermediary file format for transferring files between applications. This format lets you save an alpha channel with the file. The PICT format is especially effective in compressing images that contain large, flat areas of color. This compression can be dramatic for alpha channels, which often consist of large, flat areas of black and white.

1 Choose File > Open. Locate and open the Lesson11 folder; then select the Fern.psd file, and click Open.

2 Choose File > Save As. For file format, choose PICT File, and click Save.

3 In the PICT dialog box, specify a resolution of 16 bits (thousands of colors) per pixel or 32 bits (millions of colors) per pixel.

4 If you choose the 32-bit option, select a JPEG compression option; for more information about this option, see the previous section, "Saving in the JPEG file format" on page 224.

5 Click Save to save the file.

Note: For Windows, no JPEG options are available.

Saving TIFF files

The Tagged-Image File Format (TIFF) is used to exchange files between applications and computer platforms, such as Macintosh and IBM PC-compatible computers. The TIFF format supports LZW compression, a *lossless* compression scheme that compresses images without discarding data.

1 Choose File > Save a Copy.

2 In the Save dialog box, for Format choose TIFF, then click Save. The TIFF Options dialog box appears.

3 Choose a TIFF preview option for either the Macintosh or an IBM PC-compatible computer.

4 If desired, click the LZW Compression check box to compress the file automatically to a smaller size without losing data.

Note: Adobe Photoshop reads and saves captions in TIFF files. This feature is of particular use with the Associated Press Picture Desk system, which uses the same TIFF caption fields. To access the captions, choose File > File Info.

5 Click OK to save the file; then choose File > Close to close the file.

Saving images with alpha channels

Some file formats automatically save an image with an alpha channel. Some applications let you make use of the alpha channel when you import the image into the application. For example, you can import a Photoshop image containing an alpha channel into Adobe Premiere or Adobe AfterEffects and then use the alpha channel as a mask. Defining the alpha channel as a mask lets you create effects like playing a movie through a selected area of an image.

1 Choose File > Open, locate the Frame.psd image, and click Open.

2 Click the Channels palette tab to open the Channels palette. Channel #4 is the extra channel in the image, containing the shape of the opening of the frame.

When the image is imported into Adobe Premiere, the black area in the alpha channel will be interpreted as a mask, allowing a movie to play through the opening in the frame.

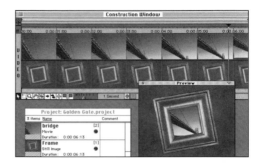

If you haven't created an alpha channel before working with this lesson, see Lesson 7, "Masks and Channels," for more information.

Choose File > Close to close the Frame.psd file. Do not save changes.

You've completed this lesson. Keep in mind that the file format you select when you save a Photoshop image must be supported by the application into which you want to import the file.

Review

• How do you determine which file format to use when saving an image for use in another application?

• What is lossy compression? What is lossless compression?

• What is the difference between the Save As and Save a Copy commands?

12

Lesson 12

Preparing Images for Web Publication

The file formats and compression options you choose for images to be distributed on the World Wide Web are determined by the image type. For example, a full-color image is saved with a different file format than a flat-color image. When preparing images for distribution on the Web, the goal is to create the smallest file possible that still maintains the integrity of the image.

This lesson shows you how to do the following:

• Determine which file formats and compression options are appropriate for publishing specific types of images on the Web.

• Prepare four types of images for distribution on the Web.

• Use the Actions palette to record a series of commands, and then run the action list on a series of files to prepare them for Web distribution.

Restoring default preferences

Before starting this lesson, delete the Adobe Photoshop Preferences file to restore the program's default palettes and command settings. For step-by-step instructions about how to delete the preferences file, see "Restoring default preferences" on page 4. After you've deleted the preferences file, restart Adobe Photoshop.

Preparing images for the Web

This lesson shows you how to prepare four different types of images for distribution on the World Wide Web—a grayscale image, a flat-color image, a full-color image, and an image containing a gradient. It is not intended to show you how to serve images to the Web.

When preparing images for distribution on the Web, keep in mind that the smaller the image, the faster the download time. However, it's also important that your image look good, so the trick is in maintaining the quality of the image while keeping the file size at a minimum.

For future reference, the following table shows which file formats and color modes should be used when preparing specific types of images for online distribution.

Image	Color Mode	File Format
Flat color	Indexed color	GIF
Full color (continuous tone)	RGB or Grayscale	JPEG
Gradient	RGB or Grayscale	JPEG
Grayscale	Grayscale	Export GIF89a
Black and White	Bitmap	Export GIF89a

Turning off image previews

One of the ways you can reduce the size of images for the Web is to turn off the Image Preview option in the Preferences dialog box. Turning off the Image Preview option saves files without a preview icon.

1 Choose File > Preferences > Saving Files.

2 Choose Never Save from the Image Previews menu; then click OK.

Note: If you throw away your Preferences file, you will have to reselect the Image Preview option.

Preparing a flat-color image for the Web

For best results, flat-color images should be converted to Indexed Color mode, and then saved as GIF files. Flat-color images appear best on the Web without any *dithering*—mixing colors to approximate those not present in the image.

You'll prepare a flat-color image of a map.

1 Choose File > Open. Locate and open the Lesson12 folder, select the Africa.psd file, and then click Open.

2 Choose File > Save As, name the file Africa2.psd, and click Save.

3 Note the file size of the image before continuing.

You'll start by converting the flat-color image to Indexed Color mode. The Indexed Color mode converts 24-bit images to 8-bit images, which display up to 256 colors (or shades of gray). If the original image has more than 256 colors, all but 256 of the colors are removed from the image. If the original image contains fewer than 256 colors, the palette defaults to Exact and the number of colors in the image appears in the text box.

4 Choose Image > Mode > Indexed Color to convert the RGB image to Indexed color.

The Indexed Color dialog box appears, where you set options for the color values and the number of colors used to display the image.

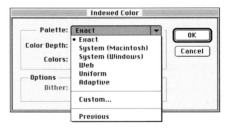

The Palette menu in the Indexed Color dialog box lets you select a color palette option, which determines the colors used to display your image.

• The Exact option uses exactly the same colors for the palette as those that appear in the RGB image. No dithering option is available for the Exact palette, because all the colors in the image are present in the palette. The Exact option is available only if 256 or fewer colors are used in the RGB image.

• The System (Macintosh or Windows) option builds a color table using the color table of the system you select. It is an 8-bit palette, capable of displaying 256 colors.

The Web palette is a cross-platform 8-bit color palette. Use this palette option if you plan to display more than one image on a page—for example, side-by-side images—so that all the images are composed of the same colors on any platform.

• The Adaptive option builds a color table using the colors from your image. If you're displaying one image at a time, choose the Adaptive palette option.

5 For Palette, select Web.

The Color Depth menu lets you select how many colors you want to use to display the image.

6 For Dither, select None. (Dithering makes the flat color look spotted.)

Note: When the Dither option is set to None, colors in the image shift to the nearest color. Keep this in mind when designing your flat-color images.

7 Click OK to apply the color mode change to the map image.

8 If desired, choose Edit > Undo; then choose Image > Mode > Indexed Color again.

9 Choose File > Save As. Name the file Africa.gif, for format choose CompuServe GIF, and then click Save.

10 In the GIF Options dialog box, select Normal for Row Order; then click OK.

11 To see how the file size of the.gif image differs from the original image, use one of the following methods:

• Choose File > Open, select the filename from the list of files, but do not click Open. The size of the selected file is displayed below the list of filenames. Click Cancel to exit the Open dialog box.

• Quit Photoshop and return to the desktop; then compare the size of the original file to the .gif file.

In this case, the original map file was about 96K, and the .gif map file is about 64K.

12 Choose File > Close, do not save changes.

Preparing a grayscale image for the Web

Grayscale images should be converted to RGB mode and then exported to the GIF89 export module. By converting a grayscale image to RGB mode, the GIF89a Export module lets you select the number of colors (in this case, shades of gray) you want to use to display the image.

1 Choose File > Open. Locate and open the Lesson12 folder, select the Hands.psd file, and then click Open.

First, you'll convert the hands image to RGB Color mode.

2 Choose Image > Mode > RGB Color.

Once you've changed the grayscale image to RGB mode, you use the GIF89a Export module to select the number of grays you want the image to display.

3 Choose File > Export > GIF89a.

Note: *If the GIF89a dialog box doesn't appear, make sure that the GIF89a Export module is installed in the Import/Export folder in the Plug-ins folder, and then restart Adobe Photoshop.*

When you export an RGB image to GIF89a format, the image is converted to indexed color (which displays an 8-bit color preview).

4 In the GIF89a Export dialog box, deselect the Interlaced option to minimize the file size.

The Interlaced option displays a large file as a low-resolution proxy first, and then redraws it at a higher resolution as it downloads it from a Web server. (In this case, you don't need to use interlacing because the file you're working with is small enough to download quickly.)

5 Click Preview to see a preview of the hands image.

6 Click OK to return to the GIF89a Export dialog box.

7 Now, to reduce the number of grays used to display the image, select Adaptive from the Palette menu and enter 32 for Colors.

8 Click Preview to display a preview of the hands image again using 32 shades of gray instead of the default value of 256 shades of gray. You'll notice that there isn't much difference.

9 Experiment by selecting different values from the Colors menu and then clicking Preview to see how the image is affected.

When working with grayscale images, you can usually use fewer than 256 shades of gray without significantly affecting the display quality of the image. Reducing the number of grays used to display a grayscale image reduces the file size, thus speeding download time on the Web. See illustration 12–1 in the color section for samples of file size versus image quality.

10 When you've decided how many shades of gray you want to use to represent the hands image, click OK to close the GIF89a Export dialog box. The Save dialog box appears with the current filename and a .gif extension.

11 Name the file Hands2.gif (for the Macintosh, remove the .psd extension from the filename), and click Save to save the image.

12 To see the difference between the original file and the .gif file you just saved, choose File > Open, open the Hands2.gif file and align it next to the original file. The difference between the two images is minimal.

13 Choose File > Close to close both files, and do not save changes.

Preparing a full-color image

Full-color images should be saved as JPEG files. The compression option you use determines how the color information in the image is preserved and the overall size of the file.

You'll save two copies of an identical RGB image as JPEG files using two different compression options. After you've saved the images, you'll close and then reopen them to compare the differences in file size and image quality.

1 Choose File > Open. Locate and open the Lesson12 folder, select the Lion.psd file, and then click Open.

2 Choose File > Save As. In the Save As dialog box, name the file Lionlow.jpg. Select JPEG from the format menu (Macintosh) or the Save As menu (Windows), and then click Save.

Now you'll experiment with JPEG compression settings.

3 In the JPEG Options dialog box, drag the slider to the left to Small File to select the Low quality compression. Click OK.

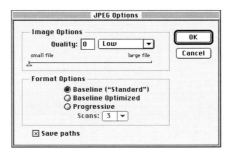

4 Choose File > Close to close the Lionlow.jpg file.

5 With the Lion.psd file still open, repeat step 2, but this time, save the file as Lionhi.jpg.

6 In the JPEG Options dialog box, drag the slider all the way to the right to Large File select Maximum quality compression. Click OK.

```
                 JPEG Options
  ┌ Image Options ─────────────────┐   ┌──────┐
  │   Quality: [10] [Maximum  ▼]   │   │  OK  │
  │  small file        large file  │   └──────┘
  │                          △     │   ┌──────┐
  ├ Format Options ────────────────┤   │Cancel│
  │   ● Baseline ("Standard")      │   └──────┘
  │   ○ Baseline Optimized         │
  │   ○ Progressive                │
  │      Scans: [3 ▼]              │
  ├────────────────────────────────┤
  │ ⊠ Save paths                   │
  └────────────────────────────────┘
```

7 Choose File > Close to close the Lionhi.jpg file.

Now you'll compare the size and quality of the two images. Before you open the files, you'll check their size in the Open dialog box.

8 Choose File > Open. Locate the Lionlow.jipg image and select it in the file list. The size of the file is displayed at the bottom of the dialog box (about 63K).

9 Next, select the Lionhi.jpg image and note its file size (about 192K).

10 Now, open both the Lionlow.jpg image and the Lionhi.jpg file, and compare the differences between the quality of the images.

You'll probably notice a difference in image quality around the eyes and nose of the lion, but because the files are small, the difference in image quality is not substantial. In general, your choice of JPEG options will depend on your image size and quality needs.

11 Close all the open files and do not save changes.

Preparing an image containing a gradient

Images containing gradients should be saved to JPEG format. For gradients, the JPEG format produces a smaller file than the GIF format with an Adaptive palette. (In addition, saving a gradient to GIF format may cause banding in the gradient.)

Now you'll work with an image containing a gradient.

1 Choose File > Open. Locate and open the Lesson12 folder, select the Economy.psd file, and then click Open.

2 Choose Image > Duplicate, name the copy Gradlow.jpg, and click OK.

3 Repeat step 2, this time naming the copy Gradhi.jpg, and click OK.

You'll select two different compression options for these images.

Close the original Economy.psd file.

4 Align the Gradlow.jpg and Gradhi.jpg images side-by-side.

5 Click the Gradlow.jpg window to make it active; then choose File > Save As. For format, choose JPEG, and click Save.

6 In the JPEG Options dialog box, drag the slider to the left to select Small File/Low, and then click OK.

7 Click the Gradhi.jpg window to make it active; then choose File > Save As. For Format, choose JPEG, and then click Save.

8 In the JPEG Options dialog box, drag the slider to the right to select Large File/Maximum, and click OK.

9 Before continuing, close both images. You must reopen them to compare the difference in image quality.

10 Choose File > Open. In the Lesson12 folder, open the Gradhi.jpg and Gradlow.jpg images and align them side-by-side.

Compare the quality of the gradient in both images. You'll notice that the quality of the gradient saved with Large File/Maximum compression is significantly better than the image saved with Small File/Low compression.

Select the Medium, High, or Maximum compression options for images containing gradients; these options preserve most of the color information in the gradient.

11 Close the files and do not save changes.

Saving an image with transparency

You can create transparent areas in an image using the GIF89a Export module. To define areas as transparent, you must first convert the image to Indexed Color mode.

You'll define the edges of an image as transparent to create a soft-edged effect around the image.

1 Choose File > Open, locate the Lesson12 folder, then select the Zebra.psd file from the list of files and click Open.

2 Choose Image > Mode > Indexed Color. For Palette, choose Web, and for Dither, choose Diffusion; then click OK.

3 Before continuing, select the zoom tool in the toolbox, and zoom in on a corner of the zebra image.

Notice the solid gray background outside the scalloped edges of the image. This gray area is the area you'll define as transparent, so that only the scalloped edges are visible when the image is opened in a Web browser.

4 Choose File > Export > GIF89a Export.

5 In the GIF89a Export dialog box, double-click the hand tool (within the GIF89a Export dialog box) to see the entire image in the preview window.

6 Click the eyedropper tool in the GIF89a Export dialog box. You'll use it to select the colors you want to make transparent.

7 Drag the eyedropper tool in the gray border area to select the pixels you want to make transparent.

The gray you selected to be transparent is outlined in the color swatches below the preview of the zebra. Also notice that other areas of the image containing the same gray colors are made transparent. However, you can correct this using a selection mask, which you'll look at in a moment.

You can confine the transparent areas to the gray in the border by loading a mask saved in a channel (which, in this case, we added in the original image).

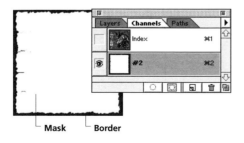

Mask   Border

8 In the GIF89a Export dialog box, choose #2 from the Transparency From menu to select the selection mask (added to the image earlier).

Notice that now the transparency appears only in the border, and the rest of the image is not affected. This is because the mask hides the image so that only the border area can be selected.

Now, you'll have a chance to change the background color in the image preview to match the background color of your Web browser. Changing the background color lets you see exactly how the image will appear in your Web browser.

9 Click the Transparency Index Color (Macintosh) or the Transparency Preview Color (Windows) swatch. (By default, this swatch matches the background color of the Netscape® Navigator browser—that is, about 192 red, 192 green, and 192 blue.)

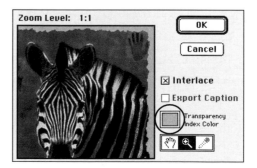

10 Select a color that matches the background color of your Web browser. (For this example, try selecting a color that isn't present in the image so that the result is obvious.) Click OK.

The image is displayed on the background color with the transparency settings.

11 Click OK to close the GIF89a Export dialog box. The Save dialog box appears.

12 Enter a filename with a .gif extension, and click Save to save the image.

The image appears to be unaffected by the transparency settings—you won't see the transparent areas around the border of the image until you open it in a Web browser.

Note: Because different users select different background color preferences, your image edges may not appear transparent on all browsers. In addition, your browser must support transparent GIF file format.

13 Choose File > Close to close the file.

Using the Actions palette to automate tasks

The Actions palette lets you automate repetitive tasks by recording and then playing back a series of commands on a single file or on a series of files in the same folder. Each set of commands is called an *action*.

Action

Although this lesson won't show you all the ways you can use Actions, you'll get a basic understanding of how the Actions palette works. For complete information about all the Actions palette options, see Chapter 15, "Automating Tasks," in the *Adobe Photoshop User Guide.*

Recording actions

When you create an action, Photoshop records the commands you choose, in the order you choose them. Not all commands and functions can be recorded, but you can insert nonrecordable commands using the Insert Menu Item command in the Actions palette.

In this lesson, you'll create an action for a series of files, called a *batch process*. Let's assume the following scenario: You have four images, originally prepared for print, that you now want to prepare for distribution on the Web. You will automate the task of changing the size and resolution of the images, the color mode of the images, and the file format of the images.

1 Choose File > Open, locate and open the Lesson12 folder, then open the folder named Images within the Lesson12 folder. Select the Crocodil.psd image from the list of files, and click Open.

You must have a file open to record an action.

2 Click the Actions palette tab. (If the Actions palette is hidden, choose Window > Show Actions.)

3 Select New Action from the Actions palette menu.

4 In the Actions dialog box, type the name **Web Specs**, and click Record. The Action name appears in the Actions palette, below the default action names.

At the bottom of the Actions palette, the Record icon becomes red, indicating that recording has begun.

5 Choose Image > Image Size. In the Resolution text box, enter **72** (Macintosh) or **96** (Windows). For Web publication, the resolution need not be higher than the screen resolution.

6 For the Pixel Dimensions, enter **100** in the Width and Height text boxes. All of the images in the batch process will be resized to these dimensions.

7 Click OK to continue. Notice that the Image Size command appears in the Actions palette.

8 Choose Image > Mode > Indexed Color. Choose Web from the Palette menu, and then click OK to continue. Now the Convert Mode command appears in the Actions palette.

Now you'll insert a menu command. You insert menu commands when you don't want to record values for a command. For example, you would insert a menu command for the Save As command, because you don't want files saved repeatedly with the same name. By inserting a Save As menu command, the Save dialog box is displayed at the end of each sequence of actions, letting you enter a discrete name and file format for each file in the batch.

9 Choose Insert Menu Item from the Actions palette menu.

10 When the Insert Menu Item dialog box appears, choose File > Save As. The words Save As appear in the Menu Item dialog box, but no filename is entered. Click OK. The Save command is added to the Actions list.

At this point, you've recorded all the commands you need for the Web action list.

11 Stop recording in either of the following ways:

• Click the Stop button at the bottom of the Actions palette to stop recording.

• Choose Stop Recording from the Actions menu.

Before you play back the action list on the remainder of the files, take a moment to look at the Actions palette.

In the Actions palette, click the triangle next to the Image Size action. The command is expanded to show all the parameters you set for the Image Size command.

Notice that no triangle is present next to the Save command, because no parameters have been set. When the action reaches the Save command, you'll be prompted to enter a name for the file. In this way, you don't accidentally overwrite files.

12 Choose File > Close to close the Crocodil.psd file before continuing. Do not save changes.

Playing back an action

Once you've recorded an action, you can play it back on a single file or on a folder of files. You use the batch feature to play back an action on a folder of files. In this lesson, you'll run the action on the four files you want to prepare for Web publication.

For information about all of the playback options you can use with actions, see Chapter 15, "Automating Tasks," in the *Adobe Photoshop User Guide.*

1 From the Actions palette menu, choose Batch. The Batch dialog box appears.

2 In the Batch dialog box, make sure that Folder is selected for Source; then click Choose to select the folder containing the files.

3 In the Lesson12 folder, select the Images folder, and then click the Select "Images" button at the bottom of the dialog box.

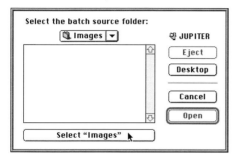

4 Choose Web Specs from the Action palette menu; for Destination, choose Folder.

Note: When you're saving to a destination folder, the folder must be created before it can be selected as a destination.

For this lesson, we created a destination folder named NewImage in the Lesson12 folder.

5 Click the Choose button; select NewImage in the Lesson12 folder, and then click Select "NewImage" at the bottom of the dialog box to define the destination folder for the new files.

6 Click OK to begin executing the action. Each of the images in the Images folder is opened; and the size, resolution, and color mode of each image is edited, based on the parameters you set while recording the action.

7 When the Save dialog box appears, for Format, Compuserve GIF, add a .gif extension to the image, and then click Save.

8 In the GIF Options dialog box, accept the default of Normal and click OK to save the file and continue.

A copy of each image is saved in the NewImage folder.

9 If desired, open the NewImage folder after you've played the Web Specs action to see how the images were adjusted.

You've completed this lesson. Now take a few minutes to review what you've learned and to think about ways you might use these techniques in your own work.

Review

• What determines the file format you should use when saving images for Web publication?

• What is the benefit of selecting the Web palette when preparing images for publication on the World Wide Web?

• How might you use Actions in your own work to expedite repetitive tasks?

13

Lesson 13

Creating Color Separations

Calibration is a two-step process that begins with stabilizing your monitor to ensure a consistent display of on-screen color. Later when you print your images, you calibrate, or define parameters for, the output device you're using to ensure a close match between the on-screen colors and the printed colors.

In this lesson, you'll learn to:

• Examine the differences between on-screen colors and printed colors.

• Create a color separation in Adobe Photoshop, the process by which the colors in an RGB image are distributed to the four process ink colors: cyan, magenta, yellow, and black.

• Understand how images are prepared for printing on-press.

Restoring default preferences

Before starting this lesson, delete the Adobe Photoshop Preferences file to restore the program's default palettes and command settings. For step-by-step instructions, see "Restoring default preferences" on page 4.

On-screen versus printed colors

Colors on a monitor are displayed using combinations of red, green, and blue light (called RGB), while printed colors are created using a combination of four ink colors—cyan, magenta, yellow and black (called CMYK). These four inks are called *process colors* because they are the standard inks used in the four-color printing process. See illustrations 13–1 and 13–2 in the color section of this book for samples of channels in both RGB and CMYK images.

Based on a variety of factors, such as changes in lighting, the temperature of the monitor, and the phosphors used to display the color, colors may vary from monitor to monitor. That is why it's important to calibrate your monitor so that your on-screen colors are consistently displayed. In a similar way, each output device outputs CMYK colors in a slightly different way, and thus printing the same image to two different output devices may yield different results. As a result, you *must* set parameters for the device to which you are printing, thereby ensuring a close match between your on-screen colors and your printed colors.

What does calibration do?

Calibration has two purposes—to stabilize the display of the colors on your monitor and to ensure a close match between your on-screen colors and your printed colors.

In Lesson 3, "Calibrating Your Monitor," you learned to calibrate your monitor. In this lesson, you'll learn to calibrate your output device by setting options that control how colors are printed on-press. Because each device has a slightly different way of displaying printed color, it's very important to follow these steps before printing, or you may be very surprised at how much the printed colors vary from the on-screen colors.

In Adobe Photoshop, three commands control the way CMYK images are separated onto the four color plates: Monitor Setup, Printing Inks Setup, and Separation Setup.

Let's take a moment to look at the function of each of these commands before continuing.

• The Monitor Setup command accounts for factors affecting the monitor display: the target gamma and white points, the type of phosphors in the monitor, and the room lighting conditions. The command also controls how the program converts colors between the RGB and CMYK color modes.

Note: You've already defined Monitor Setup options while calibrating your monitor in Lesson 3, "Calibrating Your Monitor."

• The Printing Inks Setup command lets you specify the properties of the inks and paper stock you will use. Based on these properties, Adobe Photoshop defines the value for *dot gain.* Dot gain is the change in the size of the halftone dots caused by absorption of ink (or lack thereof) on the selected paper stock, and which results in the printing of darker tones or colors than expected.

• The Separation Setup command provides options that let you define the total ink limit and determine the percentage of black ink that should be used in conjunction with cyan, magenta, and yellow to produce the richest colors. You'll learn more about this later.

These parameters must be set *before* converting an image to CMYK mode, the process by which a color image is separated onto the four color plates for printing. If you set

these parameters *after* converting an image to CMYK mode, they will have no effect on the image when it is printed.

Preparing images for print

The most common way to output images is to produce a negative image on film, and then transfer the image to a printing plate that will be run on a press.

To print a continuous-tone image, the image must be broken down into a series of dots. These dots are created when you apply a *halftone screen* to the image. The dots in a halftone screen control how much ink is deposited at a specific location. The varying size and density of the dots create the optical illusion of variations of gray or continuous color in the image.

A printed color image consists of four separate halftone screens—one each for cyan, magenta, yellow, and black (the four process ink colors).

Preparing a color separation in Adobe Photoshop

In Adobe Photoshop, preparing a color separation consists of the following process:

• Entering parameters in the Printing Inks Setup dialog box to specify properties of the inks and paper stock that the output device will use; and entering settings in the Separation Setup dialog box to control how the CMYK plates are generated.

• Converting the image from RGB mode to CMYK mode to apply the printing inks and separation setup values to the image and to separate the colors in the image onto the four process color plates.

• Setting the line screen at which the image will be printed, either in Photoshop or in the page layout program from which you're going to print.

Entering settings for printing inks

You'll begin the color separation process by setting parameters in the Printing Inks Setup dialog box.

1 Choose File > Open. Locate and open the Lesson13 folder; then select Start13.psd and click Open.

2 Choose File > Color Settings > Printing Inks Setup.

For this exercise, you'll use the default printing ink settings. When you're doing your own work, you'll probably change the values in this dialog box depending on the device you're printing to and the requirements of the individual project.

3 For Ink Colors, make sure SWOP (Coated) is selected.

Standard Web Offset Proofing (SWOP) inks printed on coated paper are the most commonly used inks in the United States. (These inks differ slightly from those used in Europe.)

4 For dot gain, make sure that 20 is entered.

The default dot gain for SWOP is 20%. This value compensates for the tendency of dots to print larger than they should on-press, and thus creating darker tones or color than expected. Different printers and papers have different dot gains.

(Always consult with your print shop technician to determine which inks to select and what dot gain value to enter.)

Important: Select the Dot Gain for Grayscale option only if you're working in a grayscale image or a duotone image.

5 Click OK.

Entering separation setup options

The Separation Setup options (along with the Printing Inks settings) control how CMYK plates are generated. Again, for this exercise you'll accept the default settings as you learn about the various separation options.

Printing black

The options in the Separation Setup dialog box let you determine how black is printed. There are two methods used to add black ink instead of mixing colors to get black ink on press: undercolor removal (UCR) and gray component replacement (GCR). This lesson briefly describes both methods. For complete information about all options for each method, see Chapter 5, "Reproducing Color," in the *Adobe Photoshop User Guide*.

The method you should use is determined by the paper stock you use and the requirements of the print shop.

Undercolor removal (UCR)

Theoretically, 100% of cyan, magenta, and yellow create black. However, this combination generates 300% of the inks in one place on the paper and creates a muddy brown instead of a true black. To compensate for this, printers remove some of the cyan, magenta, and yellow (hence the term *undercolor removal*) in areas where the three colors overlap, and add black ink.

Gray component replacement (GCR)

The GCR method of adding black ink differs from the UCR method by distributing more black ink over a wider range of colors. As a result, GCR separations tend to reproduce dark, saturated colors somewhat better than UCR separations, and also maintain gray balance better on-press.

Note: Check with your print shop technician to determine which type of separation to use.

1 Choose File > Color Settings > Separation Setup.

By default, Adobe Photoshop uses the GCR separation type.

2 Take a moment to select each option in the Black Generation menu, starting with the None option.

When you select the None option, you'll notice that the black line (indicating the percentage of black ink) completely disappears from the graph, indicating that no black ink will be added to the cyan, magenta, and yellow values to generate black ink.

Each time you select another option from the menu, you'll notice that the black line increases, indicating that more black ink is being added to the image.

3 Finally, select the Maximum option. The Maximum option uses only black ink (no cyan, magenta, or yellow ink is used). The Maximum option is useful for images that contain large amounts of solid black against a light background, such as the images of the dialog boxes in this book.

Again, fully understanding these concepts requires that you read all the information the *Adobe Photoshop User Guide*.

4 Select Medium from the Black Generation menu, and click OK.

Separating an RGB image

Now that you've entered options for both the Printing Inks Setup and the Separation Setup, you're ready, to convert your RGB image to CMYK to distribute (separate) the colors in the RGB image onto the four process color plates.

When you convert an RGB image to CMYK mode, the settings in the Printing Inks dialog box and in the Separation Setup dialog box are applied to the image.

1 With the Start13.psd image selected, choose Image > Duplicate.

2 Enter the name CMYK.psd, and then click OK to create a duplicate of the original file.

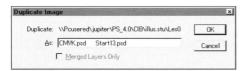

3 Align the images side-by-side so you can see both of them on your screen.

4 Make sure that the CMYK.psd image is the active window; then choose Image > Mode > CMYK Color.

When you choose the CMYK mode, Photoshop builds a color separation table based on the information you entered in the Printing Inks and Separation Setup dialog boxes. In addition, the image is separated onto the four color plates (cyan, magenta, yellow, and black).

When the image is converted, you'll notice a slight difference between the colors in the RGB image and the CMYK image. This is a natural occurrence when converting RGB colors to CMYK colors.

5 If desired, choose Edit > Undo Mode Change; then choose Edit > Redo Mode Change to see the difference between the RGB and CMYK images.

As with most scanned images, most of the colors in the original RGB image were within the CMYK gamut and didn't need to be changed. (To see a sample of color gamuts, see illustration 2-4 in the color section of this book). If the image had contained colors outside the CMYK gamut, the RGB colors would have been converted to their nearest CMYK equivalents.

You have successfully completed the process of creating a color separation for print. Keep in mind that Printing Inks and Separation Setup options only affect an image during the conversion from RGB mode to CMYK mode. Therefore, if you change these setup options after converting the image, the options will affect the display of the on-screen image but won't have any effect on the printed output.

Strategies for successful printing

The rest of this lesson provides tips and techniques to help you successfully print your images.

Working in RGB mode

The best way to create color separations is to work in RGB mode, set the separation preferences to compensate for conditions on-press, and then convert the image to CMYK mode. During the conversion, Adobe Photoshop applies the separation preferences to the image, which alters the pixel values in the image to compensate for the separation preferences. When converted to CMYK, the colors in the image closely match the original RGB image (unless you have out-of-gamut colors, an uncalibrated monitor, or both).

Working in RGB mode is faster than working in CMYK mode because RGB files are smaller. In addition, some filters and options are available only for RGB images.

Working in CMYK mode

The second strategy for creating color separations is to print a color proof to show the needed corrections, and then work in CMYK mode to make color corrections until the screen display matches the desired output.

Note: Keep in mind that even though you may have calibrated your system to create a close match between the on-screen and printed colors, you are still displaying CMYK data on an RGB monitor, and slight discrepancies in color may occur.

When you work in CMYK mode, the separation settings, such as dot gain, affect the way the image is displayed on the monitor. But because you are not converting this CMYK data to RGB mode, any changes affect only the on-screen image—the actual pixel values are not altered. For example, if you enter a dot gain of 30% while your image is in CMYK mode, the image becomes darker on-screen to approximate the dot gain, but the actual pixel values in the image are not changed. (In contrast, setting separation options on the same file while in RGB mode and then converting to CMYK mode *will* affect the actual pixel values in the image.)

Displaying individual channels

Each channel in an image provides information about that image's color values. RGB images are composed of three channels: one each for red, green, and blue. CMYK images are composed of four channels: one each for cyan, magenta, yellow, and black. You can view the individual channels in an image using the Channels palette.

1 Choose File > Preferences > Display and Cursors.

2 In the Display section of the dialog box, click the Color Channels in Color option; then click OK.

3 Make the Start13.psd window the active window; then click the Channels tab to display the Channels palette.

Notice that the colors in the RGB image are distributed in the red, green, and blue channels (the composite channel at the top of the palette shows the combined channels). For a color sample, see illustration 13-1 in the color section of this book.

4 In the Channels palette, click one of the individual channels (red, green, or blue).

5 Click the RGB composite channel at the top of the Channels palette to return to the composite view.

6 Now click the CMYK.psd window to make it active. Notice that the Channels palette now shows the distribution of the colors in the image in the cyan, magenta, yellow, and black channels. (See illustration 13-2 in the color section.)

7 To see how each plate contributes to the overall color of the final image, click the thumbnail for each of the four process colors in the Channels palette.

8 The color in each channel represents the percentage of ink used on each of the printing plates.

9 Close the Start13.psd file and the CMYK.psd file; do not save changes.

Adjusting out-of-gamut colors

Most scanned photographs contain RGB colors within the CMYK gamut, and changing the image to CMYK mode converts all the colors with relatively little substitution. Images that are created or altered digitally, however, often contain RGB colors that are outside the CMYK gamut—for example, neon-colored sportswear logos and flowers.

Note: Out-of-gamut colors are identified by an exclamation point next to the color swatch in the Colors palette, the Color Picker, and the Info palette.

Before you convert an image from RGB mode to CMYK mode, you can preview the CMYK color values while still in RGB mode.

1 Choose File > Open. Locate and open the Lesson13 folder, then select Houses.psd and click Open.

2 Choose Image > Duplicate, enter the name Houses2.psd, and click OK to duplicate the image.

3 Align the images side-by-side.

4 With the Houses2.psd window active, choose View > CMYK Preview.

Notice the difference in the two images, particularly in the intensity of the sky and the blue areas of the image.

5 With the Houses2.psd window active, Choose View >CMYK Preview again to turn off the CMYK preview.

Note: If you plan to continue editing an RGB image, turn off the CMYK preview to improve system performance.

Next, you'll identify the out-of-gamut colors in the image.

6 Choose View > Gamut Warning. Adobe Photoshop builds a color conversion table and displays a neutral gray where the colors are out-of-gamut.

Note: You can change the gamut warning color to distinguish it from the colors in the image by choosing File > Preferences > Transparency & Gamut and then selecting a new color from the Color Picker.

7 To bring the colors into the CMYK color gamut, choose Image > Mode > CMYK Color.

The gamut warning color is removed and the out-of-gamut RGB colors are converted to the CMYK gamut (using the Separation Setup and Printing Inks settings you entered.)

8 Choose File > Save to save your work.

9 Keep both images open on your screen.

Adjusting printing inks settings

You'll experiment with different separation settings to compare their effects. Two options that clearly illustrate the difference in separation settings are *dot gain* (in the Printing Inks Setup dialog box), which causes dots to be printed larger than they should for darker tones or color than desired, and *black generation* (in the Separation Setup dialog box).

You'll work with the CMYK version of the image so that your monitor will reflect the changes you make to the separation settings. Because separation settings affect only the conversion between RGB and CMYK modes, the settings affect *only the display* of a CMYK image and not the actual pixel values in the image.

1 Make sure the Houses2.psd image is active.

2 Choose File > Color Settings > Printing Inks Setup.

3 For Ink Colors, make sure that SWOP (Coated) is selected. SWOP (Coated) refers to Standard Web Offset Proofing inks and coated paper.

Note: When you produce your own proofs, you typically would get the ink type and dot-gain settings from the print shop that will print your final job.

4 Enter 40 in the Dot Gain text box, and click OK. (The default dot gain for SWOP—20%—was used to separate the Start13.psd file.)

Photoshop builds a new color table using the dot-gain setting you changed in the Printing Inks Setup dialog box. The CMYK image version now appears substantially darker, simulating what your image would look like if it were printed with a 40% dot gain. Remember that only the *display* has changed, not the pixel values in the CMYK image. If you want to change the pixel values of a CMYK image to change the way the printed image will look, you must use the Levels or Curves commands.

5 Choose Edit > Undo Printing Inks Setup to compare the effect of the default dot gain of 20% with that of the 40% dot gain you applied.

Previewing a printed image

Because of the discrepancy between the display resolution and the image resolution, the size of an image on-screen may not accurately represent its printed size. You can preview the print size of a printed image using the Print Size command.

Choose View > Print Size. The image appears in its printed size.

Important: In Adobe Photoshop, images always print from the center of the page. You cannot change the position of the image on the page to print it in a different location unless you export the file to a page-layout program.

Selecting print options

To select printing options, you make choices in the File Info and Page Setup dialog boxes, and then choose Options from the Print dialog box. The next few sections introduce you to some of the printing options; for information about all the print options, see Chapter 14, "Printing" in the *Adobe Photoshop User Guide.*

Entering file information

Photoshop supports the information standard developed by the Newspaper Association of America and the International Press Telecommunications Council to identify transmitted text and images.

On the Macintosh, you can add file information to files saved in any format. In Windows, you can add file information to files saved in Photoshop, TIFF, and JPEG formats.

1 Choose File > File Info.

2 In the File Info dialog box, type a description of the file in the Caption text box.

Note: To print a caption when you print an image, choose File > Page Setup and click the Caption option.

3 Press Tab, and type your name in the Caption Writer text box.

4 Press Tab twice, and type in the Special Instructions text box.

5 Click the Today button to enter today's date in the date box.

6 For Section, choose Origin. In the origin section, enter information that you or others can refer to later, including an address, date, and other data.

Other types of file information you can record include:

• Keywords for use with image browser applications

• Categories for use with the Associated Press regional registry

• Credits for copyrighted images

7 Click OK to attach the information to the file.

For complete information about all the File Info sections, see Chapter 13, "Saving and Exporting Images," in the *Adobe Photoshop User Guide.*

Specifying settings for different image types

The type of image you're printing, and the type of output you want, determine the selections you make in the Page Setup and Print dialog boxes.

The Page Setup dialog box lets you set up print labels, crop marks, calibration bars, registration marks, and negatives. You can also print emulsion-side down, and use interpolation (for PostScript Level 2 printers).

Printing

When you're ready to print your image, use the following guidelines for best results:

• Set the parameters for the halftone screen.

• Print a *color composite*, often called a color *comp.* A color composite is a single print that combines the red, green, and blue channels of an RGB image (or the cyan, magenta, yellow, and black channels of a CMYK image).

- Print separations.
- Print to film.

Printing a halftone

To specify the halftone screen when you print an image, you use the Halftone Screen option in the Page Setup dialog box. The results of using a halftone screen appear only in the printed copy; you cannot see the halftone screen on-screen.

You use one halftone screen to print a grayscale image. You use four halftone screens (one for each process color) to print color separations. In this example, you'll be adjusting the screen frequency and dot shape to produce a halftone screen for a grayscale image.

The *screen frequency* controls the density of dots on the screen. Since the dots are arranged in lines on the screen, the common measurement for screen frequency is lines per inch (lpi). The higher the screen frequency, the finer the image produced (depending on the line screen capability of the printer). Magazines, for example, tend to use fine screens of 133 lpi and higher because they are usually printed on coated paper stock on high-quality presses. Newspapers, which are usually printed on lower-quality paper stock, tend to use lower screen frequencies, such as 85-lpi screens.

The *screen angle* used to create halftones of grayscale images is generally 45°. For best results with color separations, select the Auto option in the Halftone Screens dialog

box (choose Page Setup > Screens > Halftone Screens) for best results. You can also specify an angle for each of the color screens. Setting the screens at different angles ensures that the dots placed by the four screens blend to look like continuous color and do not produce moiré patterns.

Diamond-shaped dots are most commonly used in halftone screens. In Adobe Photoshop, however, you can also choose round, elliptical, linear, square, and cross-shaped dots.

1 Make sure the Houses2.psd file is open on your desktop.

2 Choose Image > Mode > Grayscale; then click OK to discard the color information.

3 Choose File > Page Setup.

4 Click the Screen button.

5 In the Halftone Screen dialog box, deselect the Use Printer's Default Screen checkbox to enter another number.

6 For Frequency, enter 80 in the Frequency text box, and make sure that the unit of measurement is set to Lines/inch.

7 Leave the screen angle at the default setting of 45°.

8 For Shape, choose Ellipse.

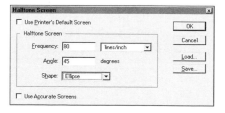

9 Click OK, and click OK again in the Page Setup dialog box.

10 To print the image, choose File > Print. (If you don't have a printer, skip this step.)

11 Look at the printed output to see the shape of the halftone dots (in this case, Ellipse).

12 Choose File > Close, and do not save changes.

13 For more information about printing halftones, see the Adobe Photoshop User Guide or talk with your printer.

Printing separations

By default, a CMYK image prints as a single document. To print separations, you select the Separations option in the Print dialog box.

1 Choose File > Open. In the Lesson13 folder, select Houses2.psd and click Open.

2 Choose File > Print.

3 Make sure that the Print in CMYK option is selected.

4 Select the Print Separations option to print the file as four separations, and then click Print. (If you don't have a printer, skip this instruction.)

The image prints as four separate pieces of paper or film. If this option is deselected, the CMYK image prints as a composite image.

5 Choose File > Close, and do not save changes.

Working with spot colors

Spot colors, also called *custom colors*, are special premixed inks that are used instead of, or in addition to, the process color (CMYK) inks. Spot colors require their own separations and their own plates on press.

Spot colors may or may not fall within the CMYK gamut; for example, a spot color may be a neon or metallic ink that is not within the CMYK gamut, or it may be a shade of green that falls within the gamut. In addition to colored inks, varnishes are considered spot colors because they also require a separate plate on press.

For complete information about how to apply spot colors to your image, see Chapter 14, "Printing," in the *Adobe Photoshop User Guide*.

This completes your introduction to producing color separations and printing using Adobe Photoshop. For information about all the printing options, see Chapter 5, "Reproducing Color," in the *Adobe Photoshop User Guide*.

Review

• How do you prepare an RGB image for print?

• What steps should you follow when preparing an image for print?

• What is a color separation? How does an RGB image differ from a CMYK image?

• How do you determine how the colors in an image will print?

• At what point does Photoshop build a color separation table?

• When you make an adjustment to dot gain in an image after it has been converted to CMYK, is the printed output affected?

• How can you affect the way a CMYK image prints without converting the image back to RGB mode and then to CMYK mode?

D

Project D

Creating Duotones

In Adobe Photoshop, you can use the Duotone mode to extend the tonal range of a printed grayscale image by substituting two or more ink colors for the gray values in the image. Throughout this project, the term duotone refers to monotones, duotones, tritones, and quadtones, which let you substitute one, two, three, or four inks, respectively.

In this project, you'll learn how to:

• Convert an image to Duotone mode.

• Load and apply a predefined set of inks to a duotone.

• Create your own ink set and adjust the distribution of the ink across the highlights, midtones, and shadows in the image.

Restoring default preferences

Before starting this lesson, delete the Adobe Photoshop Preferences file to restore the program's default palettes and command settings.

1 For step-by-step instructions about how to delete the preferences file, see "Restoring default preferences" on page 4.

2 Restart Adobe Photoshop.

About Duotones

Traditionally, duotones are used to extend the possible tonal range of black and white images on-press, which is accomplished by printing one plate with black ink and another plate with gray ink.

In Adobe Photoshop, you can extend the tonal range of a grayscale image on press by substituting one, two, three, or four ink colors for the gray values in the image, called monotones, duotones, tritones, and quadtones, respectively. Adobe Photoshop provides many predefined ink sets, called *presets*, that you can use to create duotones, or

you can create your own ink sets. See section D–1 in the color section of this book for samples of duotones, tritones, and quadtones. In addition, there are samples of duotone images with adjustments made to the color and distribution of the ink.

You can select process colors or custom colors (such as Pantone colors) for duotone ink sets. When selecting a process color for a duotone, the term process refers to any of the four *individual* process colors—cyan, magenta, yellow, or black. When you print a duotone, each ink color is printed on a separate plate.

Applying a duotone preset

You'll start this project by converting an image to Duotone mode, and then you will apply a duotone *preset* to the image. Later in the project, you'll create your own ink set, but for now, you'll become familiar with the Photoshop presets.

1 Choose File > Open. Locate and open the ProjectD folder, then select Start13d.psd from the file list and click Open.

2 Choose File > Save As, enter the name **Work13d.psd**, and click Save.

Before you can convert an image to Duotone mode, you must convert it to Grayscale mode. (If you haven't converted an image to Grayscale mode first, the Duotone command is dimmed in the Mode menu.)

3 Choose Image > Mode > Grayscale. Click OK to discard the color information in the image.

4 Choose Image > Mode > Duotone.

The Duotone Options dialog box displays the default option of Monotone, with only the Ink 1 swatch available. To the left of the ink swatch, a diagonal line, called a curve, indicates that the ink is evenly distributed throughout the shadows, midtones, and highlights of the image. At the bottom of the Duotone Options dialog box, a bar representing the distribution of inks over 256 levels is displayed.

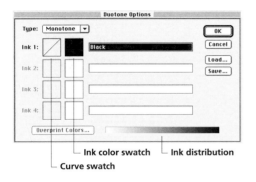

Ink color swatch — Ink distribution
Curve swatch

To select a duotone, tritone, or quadtone option, you choose the desired mode from the Type menu at the top of the Duotone dialog box.

The mode you choose determines how many ink swatches become available in the Duotone Options dialog box. For example, if you choose Quadtone from the Type menu, all four ink swatches become available.

Now you'll load a duotone preset and apply it to the image.

5 In the Duotone Options dialog box, click the Load button.

6 Locate and open the ProjectD folder, select the CK-2.ado duotone preset, and then click Open.

The ink set appears in the first two swatches in the Duotone Options dialog box.

Note that the Ink 1 swatch contains black ink. The darkest ink you use should always be in the Ink 1 swatch. Notice also that the swatch to the left of the ink colors are no longer diagonal—the curves in the preset were adjusted to change the distribution of the ink throughout the image.

7 Click the curve swatch to the left of the black ink swatch.

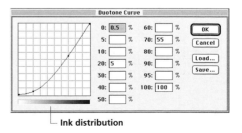

Ink distribution

The curve defines how the black ink is distributed across the image, ranging from the highlights to the shadows (as represented by the white-to-black bar beneath the graph). The curve matches, or *maps,* the grayscale values in the original image to the actual black ink percentage that will be used when the image is printed.

You'll learn more about adjusting the ink distribution using the curves when you create your own ink set later in the lesson.

8 Click OK to close the Duotone Curve dialog box.

In the Duotone Options dialog box, note that the ramp at the bottom of the dialog box has been updated to display a preview of the new ink colors.

Ink distribution preview

9 Click OK to apply the duotone preset to the image.

10 Choose File > Save to save your work.

Note: If you plan to export your duotone image to a page-layout program, save the duotone in EPS file format so that it will separate properly from the page-layout program.

Creating your own ink set

Now that you've loaded and applied a duotone preset, you'll create your own ink set. You will start by selecting ink colors, and then you will adjust the curves to adjust the distribution of the inks across the image.

1 Choose Image > Duplicate to create a copy of the Work13d.psd image.

2 Choose Image > Mode > Duotone.

To produce fully saturated colors in a duotone image, ink colors should be specified in descending order. Specify the darkest ink in the Ink 1 swatch, and the lightest ink in the last ink swatch you use. You'll leave black as the color for the Ink 1 swatch, and you'll change the ink color for the Ink 2 swatch.

3 Click the Ink 2 swatch. Click the Custom button in the Color Picker to open the Custom Colors dialog box.

4 In the Custom Colors dialog box, select Pantone 697 CV—as a shortcut, you can type 697 (If you opt to type the number, you must type quickly.)

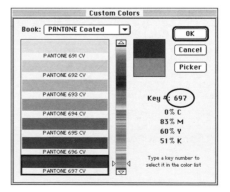

5 Click OK to return to the Duotone Options dialog box.

Adjusting the duotone ink distribution

Now that you've selected ink colors, you'll adjust the distribution of the ink using the curve swatches next to the Ink 1 and Ink 2 color swatches.

First, you'll return the black ink curve to its default value, and then you'll adjust the curve for the burgundy Pantone ink color.

1 Click the Ink 1 curve swatch (to the left of the ink color swatch).

In the Duotone Curve dialog box, note how the horizontal axis of the curve graph moves from highlights (at the left) to shadows (at the right). Also note the white-to-black bar under the curve, which depicts the tonal range of the image.

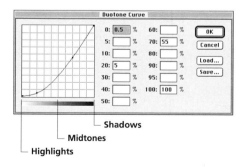

You can drag the curve to change the distribution of the ink, and you can enter values in the percentage text boxes to the right of

the graph. (At the default settings, a value of 0 appears in the 0% field, and a value of 100 appears in the 100% field.)

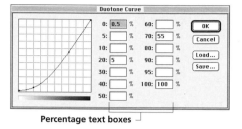

Percentage text boxes

2 To reset the black curve to its default value, drag the bottom of the curve to the bottom left corner of the graph, or enter 0 in the 0% text box to the right of the graph.

3 Remove the intermittent points along the graph using one of the following methods:

• Position the crosshair on each point on the line and drag outside the graph. When the crosshair moves outside the graph, the point is removed and the curve snaps back into place.

• Delete the values in the text boxes (but don't delete the 0% and 100% values).

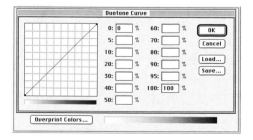

When you've removed the intermittent points, only a diagonal line remains. A diagonal line represents evenly distributed ink across the image's highlights, midtones, and shadows.

4 Click OK to close the Duotone Curve dialog box.

Now you'll adjust the curve for the Ink 2 swatch.

5 Click the Ink 2 curve swatch. You'll enter values in the text boxes to adjust the curve.

6 Enter these values in the text boxes: **30** in the 50% text box; and **55** in the 100% text box.

These settings apply a 30% ink dot to the 50% midtone pixel, and a 55% ink dot to the 100% shadow pixel, to apply less ink in the midtone and shadows of the image.

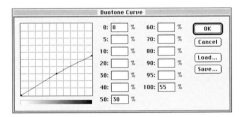

7 Click OK to adjust the curve; then click OK to apply the ink and curves to the image.

Note: If desired, you can add points to the curve and then adjust the points by dragging the point on the curve.

8 Choose File > Save to save your work.

You've completed the duotone image project. Now experiment with tritones and quadtones using your own ink colors and curve settings or the Adobe Photoshop Presets that come with the program.

For the Macintosh, the Duotone Presets are located in the Goodies folder, within the Adobe Photoshop folder. For Windows, the Duotones folder is in the Adobe Photoshop directory.

Index